I0017558

Table of Contents

Prologue

Chapter 1   Introduction

Chapter 2   What is Professionalism?

Chapter 3   The Villain Appears

Chapter 4   The IP is Stolen

Chapter 5   Legally sharing your IP?

Chapter 6   And now it becomes devious…

Chapter 7   The Detail is in the Coverup

Chapter 8   Can you trust a Retired Judge?

Chapter 9   Arbitration v Mediation – what's the difference?

Chapter 10   It is agreed upon…

Chapter 11   Tracking the Footprints

Chapter 12   And the Boot goes in

Chapter 13   The Spineless Wimps

Chapter 14   With Honesty and in good Faith – Really?

Chapter 15   … and so it ends

Chapter 16   Roadmap to Change

Chapter 17   The Final Word

Glossary / References

Appendix

Acknowledgments

The actions of the following people provided the material to write this book:

* Gary, the past President of the Association
* James, the Chair of the Complaints Investigation Committee
* Faz, the current President of the Association
* Michael, the Association representative on the Mediation
* Paul, the President Elect
* Tony, the current CEO

Thanks for an outstanding effort guys, without your work and input, this book would not have been possible.

Bruce Douglas

October 2020

Prologue

There are many Associations in Australia which represent a range of professions such as Accountants, Lawyers, Doctors, Pharmacists, Engineers, Architects, Surveyors, Journalists, etc. In addition, there are Associations based on the work domain (eg Information Technology, Organists, Ship Repairers, etc) rather than by the profession or work type.

Indeed, there are Associations for Association Executives, because Associations are big business, some with budgets of millions of dollars annually and many with a workforce to match. However, regardless of the basis of the formation of an Association, all generally have a direction or purpose focused on an area of endeavour.

Not all Associations are called "Associations" of course. Some are called an Institute (eg Institute of Physics and Engineering in Medicine), a College (eg the Royal Australian College of General Practitioners), a Faculty (eg Faculty of Pharmaceutical Medicine) and so on. Some of these Associations, Institutes, Colleges and Faculties also have a training and regulatory function which, in some cases, sets accreditation and standards of practice and professional operations.

In addition, there are also Statutory Boards (some State based) such as the Sugar Advisory Board, the Rabbit Control Board, the Surveyors Board, etc which generally operate under legislative oversight to meet their statutory function which often includes carrying out examinations and accreditation. These Statutory Board and are well regulated and scrutinised.

Regardless of the structure and / or domain focus, Associations typically have a small number of paid staff with volunteers making

Prologue

There are many Associations in Australia which represent a range of professions such as Accountants, Lawyers, Doctors, Pharmacists, Engineers, Architects, Surveyors, Journalists, etc. In addition, there are Associations based on the work domain (eg Information Technology, Organists, Ship Repairers, etc) rather than by the profession or work type.

Indeed, there are Associations for Association Executives, because Associations are big business, some with budgets of millions of dollars annually and many with a workforce to match. However, regardless of the basis of the formation of an Association, all generally have a direction or purpose focused on an area of endeavour.

Not all Associations are called "Associations" of course. Some are called an Institute (eg Institute of Physics and Engineering in Medicine), a College (eg the Royal Australian College of General Practitioners), a Faculty (eg Faculty of Pharmaceutical Medicine) and so on. Some of these Associations, Institutes, Colleges and Faculties also have a training and regulatory function which, in some cases, sets accreditation and standards of practice and professional operations.

In addition, there are also Statutory Boards (some State based) such as the Sugar Advisory Board, the Rabbit Control Board, the Surveyors Board, etc which generally operate under legislative oversight to meet their statutory function which often includes carrying out examinations and accreditation. These Statutory Board and are well regulated and scrutinised.

Regardless of the structure and / or domain focus, Associations typically have a small number of paid staff with volunteers making

Acknowledgments

The actions of the following people provided the material to write this book:

*   Gary, the past President of the Association
*   James, the Chair of the Complaints Investigation Committee
*   Faz, the current President of the Association
*   Michael, the Association representative on the Mediation
*   Paul, the President Elect
*   Tony, the current CEO

Thanks for an outstanding effort guys, without your work and input, this book would not have been possible.

Bruce Douglas

October 2020

So, the role of Directors is typically where the "stopping buck stops" because in this context the management team are only the "hired help" and while they may be sacked, rarely will they be sued.

The people responsible are the Directors. They are the ones that can be sued if something unforeseen occurs.

The "unforeseen" things that usually occur are often based around debts, malpractice, or other processes that may result in the Association (and therefore the Directors) being sued.

Debts are typically incurred with Directors signatures. Annual Reports require Directors signatures, etc. So, when a debt cannot be paid and it defaults, the Directors are (ultimately) responsible, and in many cases, they may be personally liable.

For example, should the Association incur debts of say $100,000 and then default on paying these debts without any assets to cover these debts, then most would consider that the Association is in serious financial difficulty. Should this debt remain unpaid and legal action commenced to recover this debt, then the outcome may be that each of the 10 (say) Directors could be ordered to pay their share of the $100,000 debt at $10,000 each. In some cases, this may have consequences for the Director.

An extreme example, one might say, but it has occurred.

How many people consider this when they agree to become a Director of an industry Association, I wonder?

How many Directors would be prepared to put their hand into their own pocket to pay a share of the debt incurred in their name by the Association?

up the positions of Directors, Associates, Committee Chairs, Committee members and so on.

Many people become Directors or other office holders of Associations without much thought to the obligations and consequences of being a Director or office holder, and most consider it an honour to be asked to undertake that role.

Because these are typically volunteer roles with meetings held infrequently, or in conjunction with an annual conference, the people occupying the volunteer roles often leave all of the work to the paid staff.

Mostly this is a system which works well and delivers events, conferences, training, accreditation, and a range of other functions generally in a very cost-effective (and often frugal) manner.

So, it is no wonder that the Directors of these Associations often conclude that they are not responsible. After all, the paid staff, particularly the CEO, does all the "real work" and the Directors really only "sign off" on major issues. Right?

While this may be the operating structure for many Associations, in most cases an Association is a company in the context of the Corporations Act 2001 (in Australia) of which Section 181(1) requires that Directors act "in good faith in the best interests of the corporation". In Australia, like many other countries, a Director of an organisation owes a fiduciary duty to the company and must "act honestly, in good faith and to the best of his / her ability in the interests of the company."

In some cases, Directors of Associations may be in "name only", called Directors but not holding any formal or legal authority. In these instances, some of this discussion may not apply.

But in the context of Directors of Associations which are defined within the meaning of the Corporations Act 2001, this generally does apply.

1 - Introduction

In late 2019 our company, Corporate GIS (refer Glossary Reference 1), ran a series of Masterclasses in a number of Australian cities focused on "Ethics, Professionalism and IP in the IT Industry".

These Masterclasses were based around a case study which highlighted a real-world example of ethics, professionalism and IP gone wrong.

That is, the case study highlighted what should be done and what should NOT be done.

Attendees at the Masterclasses expressed concern, and in some cases horror at the events discussed in the case study.

The participant responses expressed during these workshops resulted in a number of calls to document this case study in order to raise awareness about these issues. Delegates also considered that there was also a need to provide information on how to avoid getting caught up in a similar dilemma should it occur to them in the future. This then became the contents for this book.

A side issue resulting from the advertising and email marketing for the Masterclasses was that a deluge of emails responses were received supporting the need for these issues to be addressed. There were also emails attacking our company for running such events, seemingly from people "reading into" the marketing material that this Masterclass was attacking an Association of which they were a member. It also seemed that an Association had also received a number of attack emails from members of the community, which they baselessly ascribed to our company.

Nevertheless, the level of vitriol shown by email responses against the Association was significant and highlighted that there was a need to document this issue as a case study.

The case study discussed in this book shows how "professional" Associations in the IT Industry in Australia often misunderstand and misinterpret their roles and functions.

This book explores how easy it can be for individuals or Associations to create and follow a path of deceit and abuse of their power by trying to use other people's IP as their own.

The Case Study is about Bill and his interaction the then President (we'll call him Gary) of a major "professional" Association in the IT industry in Australia.

The reader will discover Bill's story and how Gary tried to steal Bill's Intellectual Property (IP) so that he could use it in his own consulting business.

Gary asked Bill for his IP for Association business. Both Bill and Gary were members of the Association and Gary was the President. When Gary received Bill's IP, he then quickly changed the dialogue, which was documented in a subsequent Statutory Declaration, to say that he intended to use Bill's IP in his own business, in competition with Bill.

Bill later lodged a complaint about Gary's devious behaviour with the Association, but instead of his complaint being professionally investigated, it was met with a series of processes which were designed to delay, obfuscate and whitewash the complaint. In so doing, the intent of the Association was to discredit Bill for lodging the complaint.

The reader will hear about the Association's Complaint Chair insisting that an Arbitration process be followed to resolve the dispute when Arbitration was not allowed under the Association rules. The Arbitration process was facilitated by a Retired Judge who pre-judged the complaint before all statements were lodged and without talking to the third-party witness. When asked to provide substantiation to his pre-judgement, the Retired Judge refused to disclose how he had come to that conclusion.

Following a fire-storm of legal letters from both sides, the Complaints Chair finally relented and agreed to Mediation which was the only form of resolution allowed under Association rules. But then the Association did not provide a representative who could make a decision at the mediation, thus voiding the mediation, and went on to try to whitewash the process with the agreement of the Complaints Chair.

In fact, the treatment of Bill's complaint became almost so bizarre that Bill's lawyers were left wondering at the level of incompetence of the Association.

The case study presented in this book is a true account of actual events and is presented in the context of Professionalism and Ethics in IT and Industry Associations.

This book also explores these topics in the contemporary digital world of electronic information where the lines are often more blurred than in the analogue (hard copy) world.

In this case study, you will read about the roles of Committee members and other officials for the Association. In particular, a key figure is Faz, the current President of the Association who was responsible for the process which followed after Gary, who resigned from being President, took the IP from Bill with the intention of using it for himself.

Faz appointed James to the role of Chair of the Complaints Committee and, as such, Faz was responsible for managing the actions of James during this process.

But before the story is discussed in some detail, it may be opportune to discuss the meaning of a number of these concepts, particularly that of professionalism given that the Association in this case study promotes itself as a "professional" Association.

2 – What is Professionalism?

The Merriam-Webster dictionary (refer Glossary Reference 2) defines professionalism as "the conduct, aims, or qualities that characterize or mark a profession or a professional person". It defines a profession as "a calling requiring specialised knowledge and often long and intensive academic preparation."

Professionalism

This definition goes on to state "… that professionalism encompasses a number of different attributes, and, together, these attributes identify and define a professional. These attributes are:

"Specialised Knowledge: First and foremost, professionals are generally known for their specialised knowledge. They've made a deep personal commitment to develop and improve their skills, and, where appropriate, they have the degrees and certifications that serve as the foundation of this knowledge. Not all business areas have a stable core of knowledge (and the academic qualifications that go with this); not all areas demand extensive knowledge to practice successfully; and not all professionals have top degrees in their field. What matters, though, is that these professionals have worked in a serious, thoughtful and sustained way to master the specialised knowledge needed to succeed in their fields; and that they keep this knowledge up-to-date, so that they can continue to deliver the best work possible.

"Competency; Professionals get the job done. They're reliable, and they keep their promises. If circumstances arise that prevent them from delivering on their promises, they manage expectations up front, and they do their best to make the situation right. Professionals don't make excuses but focus on finding solutions.

"Honesty and Integrity: Professionals exhibit qualities such as honesty and integrity. They keep their word, and they can be trusted implicitly because of this. They do not compromise their values, and will do the right thing, even when it means taking a harder road. More than this, true professionals are humble – if a project or job falls outside their scope of expertise, they are not afraid to admit this. They immediately ask for help when they need it, and they are willing to learn from others.

"Accountability: Professionals hold themselves accountable for their thoughts, words, and actions, especially when they've made a mistake. This personal accountability is closely tied to honesty and integrity, and it is a vital element in professionalism.

"Self-Regulation: They also stay professional under pressure. Professionals show respect for the people around them, no matter what their role or situation. They exhibit a high degree of emotional intelligence by considering the emotions and needs of others, and they do not let a bad day impact how they interact with colleagues or clients."

Do these attributes reflect the conduct of the professionals with which you work?

Could these definitions be improved for your specific business environment?

Is professionalism more of a concept than an actuality, resulting in it (professionalism) meaning different things to different people?

In their book "Professionalism in the Information and Communication Technology Industry", ANU Press, (refer Glossary Reference 3) the authors, John Weckert and Richard Lucas state "If information and communications technology (ICT) is to fulfil its potential in improving the lives of all, then the importance of the professionalism of its practitioners cannot be overemphasised. This is, of course, true of all occupations; but, there is an additional reason to highlight this in the case of ICT and other new technologies."

This book then goes on to refer to other learned works, viz: "In his paper, the Hon Michael Kirby says that Justice Windeyer, one of his predecessors in the High Court of Australia, 'once declared of the relationship between law and medical technology, that the law generally marches in the rear and limping a little'. Assuming that the situation is the same for ICT, and we have good evidence for this, we have strong reasons for emphasising the importance of professionalism in ICT. Kirby raises a number of problems in regulating technologies, particularly new and rapidly changing technologies, a central one of which is clearly ICT, and these suggest that the problem is even worse than that stated by Windeyer."

While the definition of professionalism could mean different things to different readers, it is known that the impact of professionalism onto the IT industry has the potential to be profound.

These definitions have meanings which are reasonably clear, and which should be obvious to anyone who purports to be a professional or to exhibit professionalism.

Ethics

Professional ethics are principles that govern the behaviour of a person in a business environment and like values, professional ethics provide rules on how a person should act towards other people and institutions in such an environment.

Ethics are often contained within a Code of Ethics such as the following derived from the Information Technology Professionals Association (refer Glossary Reference 4). This Code of Ethics is also used by Corporate GIS (refer Glossary Reference 1).

"Fair Treatment – We will treat everyone fairly and not discriminate against anyone on grounds such as age, disability, gender, sexual orientation, religion, race or national origin.

"Privacy – We will only access private information on computer systems when it is necessary in the course of our duties and only with prior agreement. We will maintain the confidentiality of any

information to which we may have access. We acknowledge statutory laws governing data privacy such as the Australian Privacy Principles.

"Communication – We will keep users informed about computing matters that may affect them — such as conditions of acceptable use, sharing of common resources, maintenance of security, occurrence of system monitoring and any relevant legal obligations.

"System Integrity – We will strive to ensure the integrity of the systems for which we have responsibility, using all appropriate means — such as regularly maintaining software and hardware; analysing levels of system performance and activity; and, as far as possible, preventing unauthorised use or access.

"Co-operation – We will co-operate with and support our fellow computing professionals. We acknowledge the community responsibility that is fundamental to the integrity of local, national, and international network resources.

"Honesty – We will be honest about the competence of our consultants and will seek help when necessary. When our professional advice is sought, we will be impartial and will avoid conflicts of interest and if they do arise, we will declare them.

"Education – We will continue to update and enhance our technical knowledge and management skills by training, study, and the sharing of information and experiences with our fellow professionals.

"Social Responsibility – We will continue to enlarge our understanding of the social and legal issues that arise in computing environments and will communicate that understanding to others when appropriate. We will strive to ensure that policies and laws about computer systems are consistent with ethical principles.

"Workplace Quality – We will strive to achieve and maintain a safe, healthy, productive workplace for all users."

The definition of ethics therefore describes a key set of concepts which together can be expressed as "ethical behaviour". This includes a concept of moral principles and honesty.

Are these definitions suitable for the modern world, which is often based on specific arrangements, proper project management, tight contracts, default clauses, liquidated damages, and so on, particularly in IT?

If so, how does one reconcile potential inexact notions of professionalism and ethics with modern business practices, particularly in the digital world?

Many notions of professionalism are derived from the way that some professions like to describe themselves, often in terms designed to improve their professional or social standing or to obscure the lineage of decisions that they may make.

But can this really be accepted in the digital world where most people question everything and do not assume because someone holds themselves out to be a "professional", their advice should be followed? Is the contemporary first point of reference just to Google everything in the belief that the internet is the most "authoritative" source for information?

Intellectual Property (IP)

When one extends this to IP, it has the potential to again be less definitive.

IP Australia (refer Glossary Reference 5) is the Australian government agency which administers intellectual property (IP) rights and legislation relating to patents, trademarks, designs and other rights in Australia. *IP Australia* defines IP as "… the property of your mind or proprietary knowledge. It is a productive new idea you create. This can be an invention, trademark, design, brand or even the application of your idea."

The Merriam-Webster dictionary defines Intellectual Property (refer Glossary Reference 6) as "… an idea, invention, or process that derives from the work of the mind or intellect". These definitions indicate that there are many types of intellectual property with the most well-known being copyrights, patents, trademarks and trade secrets.

As such, Intellectual Property can be considered as a creation derived from the human intellect. Most often this will be a written document (either as digital or hard copy) such as a book, but it could also include plans, designs, diagrams, paintings, etc. If the IP is a design for a new "widget" which is then manufactured and sold, it is normal for the designer to also patent that design and/or affix a trademark to protect that product from being reversed engineered after it is manufactured and is sold in the marketplace.

But it is clear that a document is IP, particularly if it is copyrighted, such as by a copyright statement on the front cover and the copyright symbol © and year included in the document, and more specifically as a footer on every page.

For example, the end product or deliverable from a project undertaken by many companies, particularly Consultants, is often a report which is presented to the client who then pays for this work. These consultancies are undertaken using time and services based on often extensive experience of the Consultant. So, does the client (or the client representative) own the report? "I paid for it" they might say, "therefore it is mine".

But while they may own the hard and soft copy of the report, they do not own the intellect that went into researching, analysing, compiling and writing the report, let alone the knowledge and experience behind all this, built up over decades of doing projects for many different organisations across many jurisdictions. That is, the Consultant owns (ie retains) the intellectual property (IP), while the client owns (simplistically speaking) the paper (hard or soft copy) containing the words.

However, if there is no "paying client" for a book or report which is provided to others for free or for a price, is there still a clear assumption of ownership?

Of course, no one who buys a book in a bookstore would assume that they own the intellectual property that went into writing the book. They are buying a book, which gives them a "right to read" – nothing more and nothing less. In the electronic world, this is the business model which is encompassed in the licensing of books available from online stores such as Amazons. One buys a "right to read" in perpetuity which expires on death. That is, when you die you cannot bequeath your Amazon book collection in your will. In simple terms, the "right or license to read" becomes null and void on death.

Digital Rights Management (DRM)

This is often referred to as Digital Rights Management (DRM) which is defined in the Macmillan dictionary (refer Glossary Reference 7) as "… control over the ways in which material used in digital formats can be used, for example making sure that people cannot copy or change it." This can be a set of access controls (software) for restricting the use of proprietary and copyrighted works.

DRM technologies generally try to control the use, modification, and distribution of copyrighted works (such as software and multimedia content), as well as systems within devices that enforce these policies.

However, it should be noted that the use of DRM is not universally accepted, and while some argue that it is necessary to prevent IP from being copied freely, others argue that there is scant evidence that DRM helps prevent copyright infringement and perhaps stifles innovation and competition.

Confused? You would not be alone.

Copyright

IP can be copyrighted, usually undertaken by making a statement declaring copyright in a prominent place on the works, such as inside the front cover of a book or in the title block of a drawing and in some cases as part of the footer on every page.

Copyright statements would typically look like:

© (Company Name), 2020

This document is Copyright to (company name). The Intellectual Property contained within this document is proprietary to (company name) and any reference to any material contained within this document must identify this document as the information source and be acknowledged to (company name).

One could also add the following:

This document is Commercial-in-Confidence. It is illegal to photocopy or electronically copy any part of this document or to distribute it outside the organisation to which it is provided.

Examples of IP and Copyright

The Surveying profession in Australia have long argued the copyright of data resulting from cadastral or property surveys (as are lodged with the various Titles Offices in Australia) rests with the Surveyor. This was confirmed by a High Court decision in 2008 following actions by the Spatial Industry Business Association.

That is, the Surveyor owns the IP of the cadastral (property) boundary survey, but the cadastral plan which results from this, and the digital cadastre derived from these cadastral plans are the responsibility of the various State Lands agencies.

Contemporary thinking is that "data" and "big data" are valuable, so it would seem that it is only right that this asset is protected from infringement and theft.

The selling of social media data to a private data analytics company in the lead-up to the 2016 US Presidential elections appeared to raise this issue to a level of social consciousness previously unseen. While most people are now concerned about who is collecting their data, where it goes, who uses it and for what purpose, they still willingly give up personal information to large supermarkets as part of loyalty programs.

This topic then becomes even more confusing when people use the work of others as a "building block" towards their own endeavours. Politeness and honesty would suggest that one would credit the source of the work that one might use, otherwise it would be plagiarism. In some cases, the lack of "source crediting" might be because they are, in effect, stealing the work that was done prior. But it may also be that they are not being dishonest, but the subject matter is so complex or the concepts so sufficiently obtuse that it is difficult to not follow on from others.

A few years ago, Apple took a competitor to court when they (the competitor) developed and sold a product which looked remarkably similar to an iPad. Apple contended that they had "invented" the iPad, that it was their IP and that their competitor should not be allowed to develop a tablet which was similar.

During the court case, it was argued the film "2001, a Space Odyssey" circa mid-80's, contained a scene where two actors were using tablets which looked remarkably similar to iPad's on a space station in the (then future) of 2001. So, had Apple invented the iPad in 2012 or had it re-used an idea from a movie in the mid-80's?

While Apple obviously invented the software used on the iPad, did it "invent" the tablet concept itself?

That is, Apple owned the IP of the software which went into the iPad, particularly the form, function, and usability of the software, but did it (Apple) invent the concept?

The court ruled that Apple did not invent the concept and therefore did not own the IP of a tablet, only the form and function of the hardware and software comprising the iPad.

So, while intellectual property can sometimes be thought of as being a bit about semantics, it (IP) can be the crux of many arguments between business people.

As such, issues relating to IP and trademarks can extend to a wide range of products and services which can be very contentious.

Trademarks

IP Australia (refer Glossary Reference 5) again defines IP as "… the property of your mind or proprietary knowledge. It is a productive new idea you create. This can be an invention, trademark, design, brand or even the application of your idea."

IP Australia then goes on to define a trademark as "a mark used to distinguish your goods and services from those of another business." In some jurisdictions, this may result in the Registered Trademark symbol ® being affixed to products.

A recent interesting example of trademark litigation shows how the "naming and typing" of product subtleties can become the source of much consternation.

McDonald's recently filed Federal Court proceedings against Hungry Jack's over Hungry Jack's new burger trademark "Big Jack", which it claims is "substantially identical with or deceptively similar" to its own Big Mac trademark.

Hungry Jack's is the owner of the registered trademark "Big Jack" which McDonald's says is "likely to deceive or cause confusion" among consumers. However, in a defence filed in the Federal Court in late September 2020, Hungry Jack's said consumers were well aware of the "competitive rivalry between Hungry Jack's and McDonald's" and it had not infringed McDonald's trademarks because consumers would not be deceived by the branding of the different products.

Hungry Jack's said if there were any similarities between the Big Mac and the Big Jack, "those similarities are common characteristics of hamburgers sold in quick service restaurants in Australia and overseas".

In this example, the name of the humble burger was considered to be IP trademarked by McDonald's which they argued was being infringed by Hungry Jack's.

IP reflects ownership of an intellect derived product or service and as such, permeates almost all business activity where products and services are bought and sold.

Probity

An extension to these discussions about IP, designs and trademarks, is the notion of probity.

While probity is particularly important for those managing contractual processes such as tender evaluations, it is a concept which is based around having strong moral principles, honesty and decency.

Probity is defined in the Australian Federal Government "Financial Management and Accountability Act 1997" as:

- The evidence of ethical behaviour in a particular process
- Complete and confirmed integrity, uprightness and honesty
- Contributes to sound procurement processes that accord equal opportunities for all participants
- A good outcome is achieved when probity is applied with common sense

- Probity should be integrated into all procurement planning, and should not be a separate consideration

Again, this is a bit of a circular argument. Ethics "relates to moral principles"; probity "relates to ethical behaviour" while professionalism enshrines rigorous ethical and moral obligations and professional standards of practice.

Are they part of a continuum or is this just being semantic?

In the case of tendering, probity is an especially important consideration. If a tender process is not conducted properly and a contract is awarded to a company on something other than fairness and "value for money", then this can be viewed as corrupt conduct.

This may, in some extreme cases, be an offence that could land the person managing the tender process in jail, which has occurred in some high-profile cases recently in Australia.

So how does one know that they have "done the right thing" in a tender evaluation apart from having a "warm inner glow"?

From having managed tenders for clients ranging from a few thousand dollars to many millions of dollars, many lessons are learnt, particularly when the evaluation of these tenders requires a rigorous process which may be difficult and tedious.

A particularly useful test is if there are no complaints about the process made by the companies not winning the tender, then the probity is probably ok.

This is because if a company suspects that their competitors are being given an unfair advantage, then they are typically very quick to lodge a complaint and demand that the process be investigated and restarted with different personnel.

So, a "working" definition of good probity can often be that there is a lack of complaint. Conversely, a lack of probity usually results in complaints and possible corrupt action.

Conflict of Interest

Another notion worth considering is that of "Conflict of Interest". This is particularly important in the case study outlined in this book because it was a conflict of interest that led to the attempted theft of IP by the (then) President of the Association.

The Ethics Centre (refer Glossary Reference 8) defines a conflict of interest as "… when two or more people (the parties) seek either:

- "the same indivisible good or benefit, or
- "part of a divisible good or benefit in an amount or in such a manner that there is insufficient in reserve to satisfy the needs or wishes of the other party or parties, or
- "where the goods or benefits that each party seeks are of such a nature that they cannot be held by those parties without giving rise to some detriment to one party or the other."

This can be further refined as a situation in which a person or organisation is involved in multiple interests, financial or otherwise, and serving one interest could involve working against another. This may relate to situations in which the personal interest of an individual or organisation might adversely affect a duty owed to make decisions for the benefit of a third party.

An interest (in this context) is a commitment, obligation, duty or goal associated with a particular social role or practice. By definition, a "conflict of interest" occurs if, within a particular decision-making context, an individual is subject to two coexisting interests which are in conflict with each other. Such a matter is of importance because the decision-making process may be compromised in a manner which may affect the integrity of the outcome.

This is particularly relevant in the context of the case study outlined in this book. A conflict of interest arises when an individual finds himself occupying two social roles simultaneously which generate opposing benefits or loyalties. The interests involved in this case study are pecuniary and clearly defined.

Typically, a conflict of interest will be addressed by the conflicted individual either giving up one of the conflicting roles or else recusing himself or herself from the situation which has given rise to the conflict in the first place.

The above definition also makes it clear there is a risk, unless remedial action is taken, that a conflict of interest can lead to corrupt behaviour, particularly when a decision (resulting from the conflict) can lead to a financial benefit to the person so conflicted.

Summary

In summary, it can be argued that:

- professionalism,
- ethics,
- intellectual property, trademarks, etc,
- conflict of interest and
- probity

… are interrelated concepts which are often expressed in vague terms and likely to mean quite different things to different people.

Nevertheless, these concepts are particularly important in modern business, particularly in the IT industry.

In the following chapters, this book explores the context of professionalism and ethics in the digital technology-rich world at the start of the third decade of the new century.

So, how should organisations and individuals behave if they seek to be "professional" and "ethical"? How does this then apply to IP, especially in the digital environment where content can be copied very easily, often without leaving a trail?

Because these concepts are often vague, it is useful to provide concrete examples of "what is" and "what is not" in terms of professionalism, ethics and IP. If one then measures their (intended) actions against a case study such as the one presented in this book, then hopefully the reader will have a better grasp about some of these vague concepts.

But first, why is this important in these industries?

While estimates vary, the IT industry in Australia is valued in excess of $100B-$150B pa of which the Spatial / Geographic Information (GIS) industry would be of the order of $15-30B pa. These are large industries where there are large amounts of money to be made by people, some by honest and professional means and some by not so honest or professional means.

The significant components of these industries usually comprise software licensing, development, services (such as integration, project management, business analysis, etc), training, documentation, hardware, and so on. Within these categories, there are large contracts to be won and large amounts of money at stake.

As such, there is often some substantial scope for people to attempt to make money by nefarious means. This could be by outright theft of technology from a competitor or by using other people's work for their own purposes, either because they do not want to do the work themselves or they do not have the skills / intellect to do the work themselves.

That is, where there are large amounts of money to be made in any industry, there will always be incentives for dubious conduct and less than ethical and legal behaviour.

The case study used in this book is one such example of an individual trying to take the work of others to use for his own purposes.

More commonly, and to use the name most people understand – this is stealing.

Taking someone else's IP and using it for their own business purposes is no different to stealing a TV from a shop or robbing a lady of her handbag.

It is most certainly not professional, not ethical nor honest.

3 – The Villain Appears

The consulting industry in IT is relevant to these discussions on ethics, professionalism and IP in IT and professional Associations because the IP that Gary attempts to steal from Bill is copyrighted "Intellectual Property" which was the product of Bill's consulting activities.

Gary is also a consultant and Gary stated in his first Statutory Declaration (refer Appendix Item 2) that he intended to use Bill's IP to further his role as a consultant.

This is a crucial issue, because this case study is about the influence that Gary's consulting activities have onto the attempted theft of Bill's IP and Gary's subsequent disregard for ethics and professionalism so as to "make good" his theft of Bill's IP.

To fully understand the Case Study, it is necessary to have some understanding of the consulting industry and how it operates, particularly in the context of the previous discussion on professionalism and ethics.

So, where abouts is Gary from, you might ask?

Gary was the (then) President of an industry Association as well as being a Director of his own consulting company.

It is usual in Associations that office holders, such as the position of President, is voluntary and unpaid, so therefore it is not unusual for such a person to be both the President of a not-for-profit Association as well as an employee or owner of a private company.

However, unless carefully handled, there are two issues which are immediately obvious as being in conflict:

- The main functions of an industry Association office holder are typically to represent Association members. Given that other Association members may work for companies competitive to the officeholder's own company, it is customary this position operates with no vested interests.
- Conversely, given the office holder is an employee or owner of a private company, he or she would at some point have very vested interests in promoting that company.

This obviously presents a conflict of interest and it is this dichotomy which gives rise to the subject of this case study.

Sadly, Gary, the villain in this story, typifies many in the Consulting industry who leave their integrity and ethical behaviour parked at the door when they try to carve out their niche as a consultant.

Consulting, particularly in the IT industry, means many things to many people, but is generally taken to mean "offering advice", in most terms for a fee.

Reputable IT Consultants provide services to clients for a fee and do so in a professional and ethical manner working under the age-old motto "do unto others as you would have them do unto you".

The Merriam-Webster dictionary (refer Glossary Reference 9) defines a consultant (not surprisingly) as "… one who consults another, and one who gives professional advice or services such as an expert."

While this is of little use as a definition, Wikipedia (refer Glossary Reference 10) provides more information about a consultant as "…a professional who provides expert advice in a particular area such as business, education, law, regulatory compliance, human resources, information technology, and so on. This person is usually an expert or an experienced professional in a specific field and has a wide knowledge of the subject matter".

Of course, in some professions such as medical, the role / title of a consultant is a rank and mostly indicates a grade of doctor.

However, most consulting in western countries in IT and related industries generally refers to someone who is employed externally to the client company and whose expertise is provided on a temporary basis, usually for a fee. Consulting firms range in size from sole proprietorships consisting of a single consultant / owner, small businesses consisting of a small number of consultants, to mid-large consulting firms, which in some cases are multinational corporations.

These types of consultants generally engage with multiple and changing clients, which are typically companies, non-profit organisations, or governments.

Because consultants generally engage with multiple and changing clients, they often have a wide range of cumulative experiences that they bring to the table for the particular project at hand. A senior consultant may bring 10, 20 or even 30 years of experience to a particular project with all the skills and knowledge from many different projects to provide a more rounded outcome from someone with a narrower focus.

In IT, Consultants are often software developers, trainers, documentation writers, integration specialists, project managers, database designers / administrators, data collectors, business analysts, change managers, etc. In all these categories of consultants, service is typically provided for a fee and, in some cases, this may include a product which is developed solely for the client to use, such as software.

It is worth noting that the Consulting Industry in general and the IT Consulting Industry in particular, is unregulated. That is, broadly speaking, there are no external adjudicators or industry Boards who regulate whether someone can call themselves a consultant or not. In many unregulated industries, one can find many "snake oil salesmen" if one looks hard enough. However, in many industries, membership of an industry body is often taken as pseudo-ratification that the Consultant knows what they are doing and has some experience, even if it is dubious experience. But because this is mostly self-regulated it is often of little worth.

A typical strategy of the "not too scrupulous" consultant is to offer advice without declaring to the client they are also taking a "kick-back" from a particular supplier or vendor to recommend a product which may be the outcome of that advice. In many industries, this would be called a bribe and become the subject of corrupt conduct ending up in jail-time for the perpetrator should such action be uncovered and proven in court.

However, the word "kickback" is often used instead of "bribe" because it sounds less illegal, in much the same manner that "shoplifting" is used instead of "stealing" to make it sound less illegal.

Of course, they all mean the same thing – shoplifting IS stealing and kickbacks ARE bribes.

Nevertheless, providing good advice to clients should include the need to declare that the consultant has no other agenda and is independent of other companies, particularly people who sell products. They should also provide a guarantee they will get advice independent of outside influences, such as kickbacks.

One such example is a company who asserted that they were independent because they sold many products. That is, they said they were independent because the customer could purchase "product x" or "product y" and so on from them. But what they did not disclose was that they received a 25% commission when they sold "product y", but only a 10% commission when they sold "product x". Therefore, it was no surprise to find they sold a lot of "product y" and very little of "product x".

Of course, they were selling products, not offering consulting advice and certainly not providing any advice independent of the product they were selling.

They were not "consulting", they were selling a product and dressing it up as "consulting" because they perceived they could make more money by doing that.

In doing so, they were misrepresenting themselves to unsuspecting clients who believed their advice was genuine when in fact it was biased to selling the specific product from which they made the most money, not the product which best met the client's requirements. Most people would regard these practices as being dubious, duplicitous or outright shonky.

Of course, it is not illegal or improper to offer advice and to sell products, however professional and ethical practice would suggest that one should disclose to the intending purchaser "your advice is intended to convince you to purchase a particular product".

When this practice is hidden, it becomes problematic and duplicitous and while this practice is not limited to companies of any genre, it is the province of the unscrupulous, unprofessional, and unethical person.

One could categorise these dubious "advice giving consultants" into the following genres:

- Duplicitous Large Consulting Companies
- Duplicitous Vendor Consulting
- Dubious Accountant Consulting
- Pretend Government / Academia Consulting

Each of these categories, including examples contained within them, are described below, to provide the context of this case study of Gary's IP theft.

Duplicitous Large Consulting Companies

A number of large companies in the IT industry have a consulting team that augments their software development team, system integration team, training team and so on. While the consulting team typically provides pre and post-sales consulting activities to assist the software development and sales processes, they often range wider and provide general consulting on the basis of helping clients to come to the correct decision.

This process then often develops into using that consulting activity as the basis of providing advice targeted to selling their software.

For example, a recent Request for Tender from a large Council near Brisbane for the development of an IT Business Case resulted in a prospective tenderer asking the following question:

"Our company has a keen interest in this opportunity and is well placed to deliver the Business Case required by this RFT and later in the project, offer our own proprietary Management System. If we were successful in being selected to deliver the Business Case, would this later preclude us from offering our software as the solution?"

The Council replied:

"... respondents should ensure their response is focussed on successfully delivering the Business Case outcomes. If a respondent is successful in obtaining this engagement, they should approach it in a candid and forthright way ensuring they deliver the best outcomes for Council. Advice provided to Council on this engagement should not be provided with a view to securing the right to engage with Council to deliver later stages."

Unfortunately, this type of activity is the norm in IT.

Companies offer to provide consulting services as a thinly-veiled cover to sell software. In this case if this company won the Business

Case consultancy, it is obvious they would not be recommending any product other than their own for subsequent implementation.

So, while the vendor in this example ethically declared this to the Council before tendering, it was clear to see the Company's real intent. When this is not disclosed, it becomes problematic and duplicitous.

Another recent example of nefarious activities undertaken by duplicitous consulting companies was that of a project involving the development of a tender specification for a major IT initiative for a large national private company. This specification was based on the work that a large Big 6 consulting company (derived from one of the "Big 6" accounting practices) had recently completed.

The Big 6 consulting company had developed the functional specifications for the major IT system but declined to write the actual tender specification or to manage the tender process because they were considering bidding on the tender.

While this was unethical and raised several "red flags", it was not uncommon in the IT industry.

That is, the Big 6 consulting company had been paid to develop the specification and then were considering bidding on the tender for which they had developed the specification. This was clearly dubious and unethical.

Nevertheless, the project to prepare the tender proceeded based on the specification developed by the Big 6 consulting company with the Big 6 consulting company bidding on the tender with a product which coincidentally fitted the functional specification which they had just written.

In addition, and on further investigation, it was discovered that the Big 6 consulting company were "business partners" with the multinational IT company for the product that they had just bid. They had been business partners for a number of years.

That is, the Big 6 consulting company, who were business partners for a major software product, had just been paid by their client to write a specification for a major new IT system based around the client's business needs, but instead wrote that specification based around the software product sold by them (the Big 6 consulting company). Then the Big 6 consulting company responded to the tender with a product that neatly fitted the specification.

The tender had a nominal budget of $6m to $10m, so it was not a small project by any means.

This highlighted a couple of issues:

- Firstly, the client should have undertaken some "due diligence" before accepting the proposal to retain the Big 6 consulting company. This due diligence should have included the requirement to disclose any conflict of interest, such as selling software that would result in financial gain for the Big 6 consulting company.
- Secondly, the Big 6 consulting company should have declared they were business partners and resellers of the software before accepting the contract to develop the functional specification.

When the client company CEO learned of the underhanded tactics of the Big 6 consulting company, and despite his exasperation over their behaviour, he allowed the matter to slide. By doing so, he telegraphed that he had little regard for probity and ethical considerations and was prepared to compromise the tender process.

Of course, it goes without saying that if the Big 6 consulting company had done this once, they were probably prepared to do it again. So how could one trust their advice again, particularly in the future when they would be promising to build more software to a fixed budget and timeframe?

By letting the Big 6 consulting company continue to be involved, it was evident that there was a high risk that this process may become a disaster.

As a precursor to the tender, an Expression of Interest (EOI) document was developed and released to the market with responses being received from suppliers. The Big 6 consulting company bid their own product, based on the work they did in the development of the functional specification. The result was that they were selected by the project Steering Committee for the tender short list.

By this time, the CEO had told the Project Steering Committee that he knew nothing about IT and had seen many IT projects fail in his previous roles in Local Government. However, he continued to direct the process and not listen to those on the Steering Committee who were skilled in this area. Again, this was a failure of due diligence and governance by both the client and the Big 6 consulting company.

The CEO then informed the Steering Committee he had hired another company of consultants, the Digital consulting company, to provide advice on the technologies bid during the EOI. This was most likely an attempt to tamp down concerns pointed out by the consultant over the specification developed by the Big 6 consulting company without disclosing that they sold software which they had bid in the EOI.

In response, the Digital consulting company reviewed all of the products tendered in the EOI and provided a positive review on the technology bid by the Big 6 consulting company, thus supporting the CEO's recommendation to continue to include the Big 6 consulting company's response. However, what was apparent after reviewing the website of the Digital consulting company was that they (the Digital consulting company) were also a business partner of the same technology which was bid by the Big 6 consulting company.

Of course, they praised the software tendered by the Big 6 consulting company because it was in their interest to have that product selected so that they could participate in potential future development for their financial gain.

Again, the CEO had not undertaken any due diligence and the Digital consulting company had not disclosed that they had a conflict of interest because they were selling that product as well. This was starting to look less like a coincidence and more like a deliberate process to empower the Big 6 consulting company to win the tender.

Of course, the Big 6 consulting company and the Digital consulting company were both positioning themselves to receive their share of the on-sell of software development and integration following the sale and implementation of the software under the contract.

Nevertheless, the tender specification was completed and proceeded to go through the Request for Tender (RFT) process. Again, all bids stated their compliance to the specified requirements of the tender.

But the consultant had suspicions about the truthfulness of some of the vendor responses. There was concern that they were bidding software which had not been developed, colloquially known as "vapourware". Therefore, the consultant suggested that the Project Manager should ask each vendor to confirm that their responses in their tender to which they said that they "complied", meant that they could demonstrate the complying functionality should they be requested to do so in the next month.

As the consultant suspected, and it was no surprise, the responses from some vendors were changed from "complied" (which meant they could meet the criteria) to "needs to be developed" as they were unable to demonstrate their ability to meet the criteria.

This showed a low level of believability from these vendors, as distinct to those vendors who kept their responses much the same and therefore could meet the criteria because it was apparent their product existed and was not vapourware.

An outcome of this process was the creation of a "believability index" by the consultant based around each vendor's credibility to meet the criteria and whether they were telling the truth or not. This was important because at some future point there would be a need to trust one of the vendors to meet their obligations under the contract when awarded.

As expected, the believability index score for the Big 6 consulting company rated the lowest, indicating that their inability to be honest in meeting the criteria showed that they were making untruthful statement and therefore could not be trusted. From any probity considerations, the Big 6 consulting company should not have been considered a credible vendor and should then have been set aside from the tender process.

However, the CEO again refused to acknowledge this information and continued to assert the process had not been compromised.

By then it was clear the CEO and the Project Manager were facilitating the tender process in favour of the Big 6 consulting company. Consequently, the consultant terminated his contract to avoid compromising his integrity.

With a tender price upwards of $10M, there was plenty of money in the pot for the Big 6 consulting company to manipulate all ethical boundaries and deceive the client.

Sadly, this process is often typical of many consulting companies who would otherwise appear to be reputable companies but have found they can make more money from selling software rather than providing professional consulting advice. In doing so they compromise the integrity of their consulting process in order to achieve higher margins of profit.

That is, they are conflating "consulting" into "pre-sales activity" under the guise of a "trusted advisor" and in this process are deceiving their clients through the non-disclosure of these unethical practices.

Duplicitous Vendor Consulting

Many Vendors also regard themselves as consultants, confusing pre-sales activity designed to sell software with the consulting process of determining client problems and providing advice, which may include software. This seems to be because most vendors regard the software that they sell as "the best" and therefore have the erroneous belief that the most appropriate way for a client to solve their problems is to buy the vendor's software.

That is, vendors often adopt a "buy my product" approach without understanding that this will not solve the client's problems, even if their software is partly or fully suitable, mainly because the problem was likely more than just a software purchase.

One of the reasons for this approach is often that many vendors believe the propaganda about their own software, exacerbated by them not knowing much about the capabilities of their competitors' systems. This is because they generally do not have the opportunity to investigate competitors' systems and it is highly unlikely that a competitor would demonstrate their system in any detail in any case. The result is that vendors are often left with believing their own glossy brochures.

As one vendor is often prone to drone; *"We are the biggest GIS vendor on the planet! why would you NOT by our product?"* But their view of the GIS market is very jaundiced and excludes other larger organisations due to specific technical market definitions.

"I could do this consulting stuff in my PJ's before my morning coffee", said Quill, a senior sales guy from one of the bigger vendors a good few years ago. He had invited me to lunch to tell me that I needed to hire him as my head consultant (and partner) because he "knew all about this stuff".

Apart from being arrogant and offensive, Quill also "assumed to know" all about consulting and our business, declining to ask questions, which is a very basic requirement for good consulting, because he already knew the answer.

So, when the bait was not taken to hire Quill, he became quite belligerent and demanded to know why I would not hire him as my head consultant.

What Quill failed to understand was that an essential trait for a consultant was listening and understanding client problems before proposing any solutions. That is very important because unless one understands the problem it is very hard to propose a credible solution.

But many vendors already knew the solution – in their mind it was "just buy my product" and all your problems will be solved. This is not true of course and is very misleading.

Of course, some vendor consulting is legitimate and mostly revolves around providing detailed analysis and technical advice about how to use their software products or to develop specialised software to provide additional functionality or to integrate systems. But this is typically undertaken by vendors for clients who have already implemented their systems and are seeking better ways of deploying or integrating software.

Another example was Lynette, a software vendor, who called wanting some advice so that she could bid on a consulting project that she "… knew that she would be great for".

It was obvious that Lynette just assumed that consulting was easy and that she knew all about this stuff. Despite misgivings that she was becoming a competitor, she was given an outline of what was required in the hope that the project would not be a failure.

"But I know all about these technologies", she said happily, assuming that this was all that was required. But what she did not understand was that knowing about all the technologies was the easy bit. Understanding the business processes, its culture, staff skills and capabilities as well as future business aspirations so that these technologies could be applied was the hard bit. It might be that that business processes did not want or need these technologies. But what would they know? Lynette was determined to sell her stuff whether it was needed or not.

So, in doing, she assumed that this consulting stuff was easy because her company developed software. It was a bit like assuming that riding a surfboard is easy because you had sat on a beach and watched a professional riding a wave. To get on a surfboard and ride it successfully without any experience and without falling off is almost impossible for a novice.

But Lynette was not to be deterred.

In her mind, she had become a consultant and used it to sell some expensive software to an unsuspecting customer and then went back to her day job. Unfortunately, her customer did not realise until much later that he had been over-sold and under-delivered.

These types of actions are indicative of duplicitous vendors masquerading at being a consultant to sell software. All of which is unethical and unprofessional.

Dubious Accountant Consulting

Many of the very large consulting companies in IT have been derived from large Accounting companies, often by forming a consulting division.

In a recent book, "Trust me, I'm an IT Consultant" (refer Glossary Reference 11), many examples are provided of consulting practices from the "Big 6" companies which were derived from the larger Accounting practices over the last few decades. Because Accountants have always been regarded as "trusted business advisers", some of the larger accounting groups have moved into the business advisory market and into IT in a more focused manner.

One of the reasons that Accountants have historically played a role in IT goes back to when computers were first introduced into companies in the 70's and 80's. In many companies of that era, the Finance / Accounting section was the group in charge of the computers because the computers were used for the financial systems, payroll systems, purchasing systems and so on, all of which were the responsibility of Accountants. So therefore, the Accountant often became the Computer Manager because they were in charge of the computers, not because they knew a lot about computers.

Over time a lot of Accountants then came to believe their own rhetoric that "because they were Accountants and managed the computer section, then therefore they were also computer experts".

This led to many a bizarre situation where a number of very large accounting practices spawned IT consulting groups on the mistaken belief that they were the experts in IT while in reality having very little knowledge of the subject.

Nevertheless, over time most Accounting consulting practices did learn about IT and hired IT people to manage their IT consulting teams. This practice was also attractive to some of the Accounting industry, because while the Accounting industry is heavily regulated, the IT industry and the IT consulting industry was not.

This unregulated landscape provided the opportunity for some of the more unscrupulous Accountants to do as they wished without recompense or oversight. Of course, not all Accountants are of this ilk, but there are some that have given the profession a bad name, as is the case with most other professions.

Pretend Government / Academia Consulting

Over the last couple of decades, the Education and Government sectors have faced budget cuts, in some cases very severe cuts, while being instructed to increase productivity.

An outcome of this process was that many groups within Government or Academia came to regard consulting as a means to "earn easy bucks" which they could then use to top up their budgets or prop up their failing institutions.

Of course, these people generally had little understanding about how to go about running a business, particularly what the appropriate rules were, because they had never worked outside of government or academia for all their working lives.

If these Government or Academic staff made a bad decision or undercut a competitor to win a tender, all that would happen is that additional government budgets may have to be spent to "bail out" the situation.   That is, for many of these staff, running a consulting business was just a side-line to make some money when they had some spare time, rather than being a serious enterprise.

Whereas a similar bad decision from the owner of a legitimate private company could result in the business owner defaulting on mortgage payments or cutting spending on their children's education. That is, running a business for a private company had serious and personal consequences whereas running a business from a government department or a university rarely had serious consequences.

So, the "game play" for many of the Government or Academic staff was to assume that no rules applied and that they could become consultants based on no experience nor any understanding of consulting processes. They just assumed that if they undercut legitimate consulting companies enough, they would win the business and make money.

Of course, the government staffer or academic only had to cover wages and did not have to consider the normal business overheads such as rent, power, staff overheads, insurances, risk, profit, regulatory costs, etc. As such, many considered that the actions of academics and government staffers undertaking consulting as a side-line were immoral and inappropriate and often backfired on them, in some cases spectacularly.

Over time the owners of legitimate consulting businesses made representations to heads of government departments and Universities, suggesting that this practise was unethical and should stop. Consequently, this practice did indeed stop as they realised that it was hard work running a "pretend business" while contending with the legitimate private sector continually complaining about their unprofessional behaviour.

An outcome of these experiences was that Governments went on to only become involved in consulting work usually when there was a market failure or when the work involved was very specialised or high-end. Of course, the definition of "market failure" was problematic given that the government departments making that assertion were the ones who were the most to blame (and had the most to gain) for undertaking dubious consulting practices.

Independent Consultants

Earlier in this Chapter, the notion of independence was discussed in some detail in the context of a Consultant in the IT industry. So, what does it mean when a Consultant says that he/she is independent?

One could define independence (in the context of consultants) as providing advice that is given free from a conflict of interest. That is, the advice is not dependent on the advice giver trying to sell a product or service and / or to convince the advice receiver to purchase that product or service, unless this is declared by the advice giver.

But industry experience is that very few IT and GIS consultants are really independent. Most have relationships with technology providers as a "partner", by commission or by a "kick-back" to recommend products or services.

In doing this, a number of Consultants use the label of "independence" as a ruse to sell a product or service to increase the consultant's revenue rather than providing advice which is focussed on meeting the needs of the client.

For example, the web site of Gary the GIS Consultant and villain of this story says his company is "strictly vendor-independent". That is, on first glance this statement would suggest that they are not biased toward any particular software product.

But a further read of the web site shows that they provide support and software development in ESRI, QGIS and Munsys. This would strongly suggest that they have skills in those 3 software products. This then raises the issue of whether any advice provided by these Consultants would really be independent or would it be biased toward one of these 3 products.

That is, would they provide advice to implement software which is not one of these three products. Or would they recommend that the client implement one of these 3 products so that they can position themselves for future development and support work with their preferred skill-set?

That is, a key focus of being "independent" is that it should be based on providing advice which meets the needs of the client, not advice which has the potential to increase the revenue of the consultant.

Summary

In summary, Consulting only looks easy because the people who know what they are doing have extensive experience doing it and because they have done it many times previously.

Again, it is much like riding a surfboard – it only looks very easy because the people doing it have a lot of experience. Professional consultants know what they are doing because they have done it many times before and have a good understanding of the process.

In some cases, some of the consulting companies have developed a methodology which defines the process which should be used and to which they assiduously follow. In my book, "Achieving Business Success with GIS", (refer Glossary Reference 12) published by Wiley & Sons, London, the BIOA consulting methodology is described which was developed by our company for undertaking business-based consulting in the high technology area of Spatial Information systems which our consultants follow religiously.

Of course, it is always useful to ensure that the consultant proposed to do the work has actually done this before, so calling previous customers and reference checking is very important, as is ensuring that the consultant doing the work is the one whose reference you are checking.

Unfortunately, a standard "game play" of the not-too-ethical consulting company is to bid a very experienced person to win the business and then to swap that person out for a junior who would actually do the work, usually on the pretext of some made-up calamity that precludes the experienced person from actually doing the work.

While it is agreed that there is a need for junior staff to get training and experience, much the same as apprentices need to get experience, that should not be at the expense of the project being done correctly.

It is true that clients are not stupid and they quickly realise that that they are being "sold a lemon" when they hire a very experienced consultant to do a major piece of work and then get a junior and inexperienced consultant to do the job, supposedly under the "supervision" of the experienced consultant back in the office (which mostly never happens of course). In some cases, the junior consultant is even charged out at the same rate as the experienced person, further annoying the client.

That is why it is always prudent to undertake due-diligence and check the references of the consultant who is proposed to do the job and then ensure that this is the person who actually does the consultancy.

After all, you're probably paying a high rate to get an experienced consultant, why should you expect less.

4 – The IP is stolen

The story of Gary trying to steal Bill's IP started several years ago when Bill received a call from Gary, who was then the President of a national industry Association in IT and GIS.

Gary was also a competitor to Bill having formed his own consulting company a year or so earlier after he was sacked from a major GIS vendor.

"Can you send me a copy of one of your industry reports", Gary said to Bill, "I have a meeting next week with the software vendor that the Association went into partnership with to produce the industry report a year or so back". "They're not being very helpful and have only given us the glossy marketing stuff from their survey and none of the underlying information which was part of the agreement".

"I'd like to use your reports to show them what a proper report should be like", said Gary.

As Gary was the President of the Association, he made it clear that he was speaking on behalf of the Association, not as the owner of his own consulting company. He initiated the conversation as the President of the Association and referenced an upcoming meeting between the Association and the vendor who they had partnered with to do the industry report.

Bill knew that this issue with the vendor was a general problem in the Association. They had been shafted by the vendor who was using the "partnership" between the Association and the vendor to get the end-users of GIS systems to part with their considerable intelligence under the guise of an "industry survey". Of course, the vendor kept all the intelligence to themselves and just released some overview material to the Association.

Therefore, the Association were feeling a bit jaded, like they had been taken for a ride. Well they should have been, because they had been.

Bill did not point out that his company had been doing these industry surveys for almost two decades and had a wealth of proprietary knowledge about how to do the surveys and what to expect from them.

When the Association went into the "partnership" with the vendor, they did not think that they were about to be used in the way that they were. They did not realise that they were just a means to an end for the vendor.

So, they (the Association) did not think that they should get a couple of competitive proposals or quotes from people in the industry who had done this type of work many times before. Such as Bill's company who had been doing industry surveys for a couple of decades and received industry accolades from doing so. The Editor of the major magazine in the industry said in a previous edition that the surveys done by Bill's company were "… the most authoritative statement available on the penetration of GIS into organisations and on the way it is being used".

So, the Association got what they deserved for not doing their due diligence and being sloppy – nothing.

The vendor got all the intelligence and the Association (and the industry) got a report that was mostly marketing material which did not contain anything of any real value. Now after being this stupid, Gary who was the President of the Association at that time, was calling Bill to try and get a copy of Bill's report to show how it should be done.

Bill thought that this was all their own fault that the Association was shafted by the vendor. Now they wanted to use Bill's reports to show the vendor how it should be done.

So, Bill provided the report to Gary in an email shortly thereafter.

Just over an hour later, Gary replied:

"It has been a while since I looked at this report. I forgot how absolutely comprehensive it was! I am considering reviving it, if you are happy to come to some IP / collaboration agreement. I don't want to steal your IP, but I also need to find a way to make it work for me. The market has changed somewhat, and I will have to change many of the parameters. But keeping things in line with the work you did will enable me to develop an historical comparison base." A redacted copy of this email is provided in the Appendix at Item 1.

Bill was incensed.

"Who does Gary think he is" said Bill "this is our work, it is our IP, we own it, I give the Association a copy of our report in good faith for Association business and then Gary says that he will just use it in his OWN company. He says that he did not want to steal our IP but then goes on to say that he intends to do just that."

"I didn't give the reports to Gary." said Bill, "I gave the reports to the Association of which he was the President, in good faith, for the Association to use in the Association's business, not for Gary to use in Gary's business."

"And now Gary's email does not say anything about it being used for the Association. Now he is saying that he will just take my IP and use it. The Association did not get a mention now. I gave a copy of the report to the Association, not to Gary for his company to use", Bill said. "To think that I supported him when he got booted from the open systems vendor and gave him advice and encouragement to start his own business. He repays that by trying to steal my work."

To say that Bill was furious was an understatement. Bill and his team at the company reportedly spent $50-100k each year doing the industry surveys, so it was a considerable investment for a small company. While they had visions of selling a lot of reports to defray the costs in the initial years, it became apparent after a couple of years that this was not going to happen.

As such, the IP had become an industry report done with participation of the industry for the industry and provided by Bill's company for no cost, because contributors received a copy of the report for free to incentivise them to contribute. In return, Bill and his company used the information for marketing and as an assist in their consulting practices.

Of course, Bill realised that a number of customer sites also illegally gave a copy of the report out "the back door" to other people in the industry but that could not be stopped. Still it was a considerable investment to gift to the industry for no cost. So this was the way that the industry Association repaid that investment – by trying to steal Bill's IP.

So, Bill sent an email back saying:

"Gary, I provided those reports to you in good faith in your role as the Association rep in your discussions with the vendor. At no time did I offer you copies of my reports or IP for you to use in the conduct of you doing a survey. Your previous email makes no mention of the Association / vendor discussions but indicates that you intend ripping off my IP for your own purposes. I find that deceitful and reprehensible.

"Accordingly, I demand that you immediately destroy any hard and soft copies of the report that I sent you earlier today and email a signed Statutory Declaration to me stating that you have destroyed all hard and soft copies of the report and that you do not intend for your survey and/or report to have any content or format which has been copied from, or is similar to, any of my reports."

After some more clarifying emails, Gary sent an email the next morning to Bill, saying:

"Attached is the Statutory Declaration. I have meetings this morning, when done I will find a JP to sign and then send back to you."

But the Statutory Declaration that Gary had attached did not include Bill's points from his email but had been changed to say:

"I have removed all copies of reports sent to me as requested. I have no digital or printed copied of any of these reports, nor do I have access to any of these anywhere. Having seen the reports, I will refer to these in my discussion with external parties, and if required will ask the individuals to contact you should they need further information." A redacted copy of this Statutory Declaration is provided in the Appendix at Item 2.

Bill was incensed. Gary was now saying that he *"will refer to these in my discussion with external parties"*. That is, he was saying that he <u>would</u> use Bill's work.

The next day, Bill responded with a demand for Gary to sign the Statutory Declaration with the words provided by Bill, not Gary's alternate words which said that he intended to continue to use Bill's IP.

Bill emailed Gary several times over the next few days as it became obvious that Gary was "ducking and weaving" and did not want to respond to Bill. Then all went quiet from Gary for several weeks, despite Bill repeatedly calling and emailing Gary. Finally, Bill emailed Gary and said that he was commencing legal action and that if he wanted to avoid this, he should respond to Bill by the end of the day.

Gary responded that he was *"…on the road and not able to respond fully. I have referred this entire matter for legal advice and will get back to you when this is done."*

It was clear from Gary's response, or lack of response, that he (Gary) was being cagey and was not going to agree to Bill's demands. He had the reports and intended to use them.

Gary had said in his Statutory Declaration that he was going to continue to have discussions *"... with external parties"* using Bill's IP.

Gary was making no mention of the Association and vendor discussions which were the point of the original request for the reports, just *"external parties"* which could be anyone, even Bill's competitors.

Bill had provided the reports to Gary in good faith for use by the Association and now Gary intended to use them in his own company and *"...if required will ask the individuals to contact you should they need further information"*.

In other words, Gary intended to be "the gatekeeper" of Bill's reports when they were not his reports to be gatekeeper of in the first place. Certainly, if there was any market advantage to be gained from the reports then it should have been to Bill's company, not to Gary's company who had done no work and spent no money creating the reports.

It was also apparent from Gary's actions, that he was being sneaky and underhanded and was engaging in actions which would be considered by most people to be bordering on being illegal.

Had Gary been honest, ethical and professional, then he would have simply signed the Statutory Declaration as requested and that would've been the end of it.

Bill would have accepted the Statutory Declaration and chalked it down to Gary:

- having made a mistake and was now correcting that error; or
- was being naive for thinking he could take someone else's work and get away with it.

Either way, it would be over and done with.

The fact that Gary persisted in his duplicity, and continued to avoid responding to Bill's emails and had sent a Statutory Declaration in which he said he was going to continue to use Bill's work, simply highlighted that Gary was being deliberately devious and deceitful.

That is, this was not a misunderstanding or an oversight – it was deliberate.

That was transparently obvious by this stage. It was deliberate and Gary fully intended to steal Bill's work.

One could go further and suggest that this was a "shakedown" which had been planned by Gary from the start by:

- using the ruse of a discussion between the Association, of which Gary was the President, and the vendor to extract a copy of the report from Bill;
- trading off Bill's good nature to extract the report; and
- continuing to use the report for Gary's own purpose.

Of course, the process also showed a lack of oversight by the Association. They either did not know how Gary was misrepresenting them in the industry or simply did not care. Either way, one could argue that they were culpable in this illegality.

This also raised the question of whether Gary had done the same thing previously. People who steal things rarely do it only once – they mostly do it a number of times, it even becomes a character trait that they do as a matter of course, even though they might only be caught once.

In summary, and to correlate Gary's actions against the previous discussions about professionalism, ethics, IP and probity as outlined in previous Chapters, it is apparent that:

- Gary's actions were not professional;
- Gary's actions were not ethical; and that
- Gary's actions could not be described in any way as being indicative of a process that had probity as a key feature.

If Gary was being professional and ethical:

- he would not have asked for, nor taken, the report under the guise / ruse of it being for the Association of which he was the President;
- when asked, he would have signed the Statutory Declaration promptly using the requested wording;
- he would not have changed the wording of the Statutory Declaration to say that he intended to continue to use the reports that he had received under false pretences; and
- he would not have requested the reports without the full knowledge of the Association, for which he was supposed to be acting.

5 - Legally sharing your IP?

In Chapter 2, Intellectual Property (refer Glossary Reference 6) was defined as "… a category of property that includes intangible creations of the human intellect. There are many types of intellectual property, the most well-known are copyrights, patents, trademarks, and trade secrets".

That is, IP is a creation derived from the human intellect and while this can be a written document such as a book, it could also include plans, designs, diagrams, paintings, etc.

Copyright on IP such as documents, books and manuscripts can be claimed by making a statement claiming copyright and affixing the copyright symbol © and year included in a prominent place in the document, generally on, or inside, the cover.

An extension to a discussion on IP is that of licensing the IP, so that a "right to use" can be granted with conditions, most often involving a payment of a fee. While Digital Rights Management (DRM) most often applies to books and other manuscripts and the licensing of them, the broader issue of licensing in the IT industry most commonly applies in relation to software licensing and data licensing.

Software Licensing

A couple of decades ago software was purchased on media, initially on tapes and disks and then on CDs. These software purchases came with a license which outlined that the purchaser was buying a "right to use" only and did not own the software. That is, the software was licensed to the purchaser, but the ownership remained with the software provider / developer. In many cases the software came with a keycode to "unlock" the software.

Often there was no time limit on the use of the software which was licensed and could be used in perpetuity without additional charges, unless the user upgraded the software, generally for a small fee. Of course, many of these licenses were not upgraded and reached a stage where they could not operate on modern operating systems and therefore had to be either upgraded or discarded.

The software which was licensed was the object code only, which is a compiled file produced when the source code (programming statements that are created by a programmer) is compiled using a compiler. So apart from running (or using) the software, the end user could do nothing else with it, which is quite different from other forms of IP which can be copied or reverse engineered.

However, as time progressed it became apparent that a number of users were providing and selling the software CD on to other people, along with the keycode. This was, in effect, stealing and was therefore illegal. But to many people this was called piracy, thought of in the guise of the software being "liberated" from the company which developed and owned the software.

During this period much the same thing was occurring in the music and movie industry. The growth of pirated music and videos grew exponentially over the last decade to such an extent that the movie and music industries put out substantial marketing programs to inform the public that "pirating movies and music is stealing". Not only was this illegal, but it was robbing the performers and movie studios of legitimate income.

Of course, piracy was not limited only to software, music and videos, it was rife throughout the digital world, but was evident in some domains moreso than others.

But because the piracy of music, videos and software was theft, the companies that owned these forms of digital data put a lot of effort into trying to stop or reduce the theft.

Microsoft's Bill Gates once opined that "… our biggest competitor is ourselves" when referring to people not upgrading software because they were satisfied with their current version. In other words, there was not a compelling value proposition to encourage people to spend money on upgrading software when the new features were of little or no use to the user, which in some cases exacerbated the piracy.

So over time, software licensing business models evolved as technology evolved. A big driver for this change was to move users onto a continual upgrade cycle (such as is the case with subscription-based software licensing) and to stop the piracy. Or at least to control and minimise the theft of software.

That is, over the years software licensing models changed from a single use license model to:

- a server-based (eg mainframe) license where the software was installed on the server and used by (often) large numbers of desktop computers across a business enterprise
- use of "corporate licenses" often with unlimited numbers of software "installs" on desktop computers across a large organisation for a single corporate fee
- the migration of the software to internet accessible platforms where users downloaded a copy of the software to their desktop for a one-off fee or a recurring (eg annual) fee
- the further development of the cloud sourcing concept to Software as a Service (SaaS) model where users accessed the software in real-time from the cloud for a time-based fee (eg monthly) or a service-based fee (eg on a per use basis).

In addition, there were other licensing models employed from time to time. Some GIS vendors such as MapInfo and later ESRI used a license model based on the size of an organisation, mainly targeted at Local Governments. This was a particularly useful model whereby Councils could have access to all of the vendor's range of software (which they might not otherwise be otherwise able to afford) based on the number of ratepayers. For smaller Councils this was a very attractive offer.

Data Licensing

The provision of data, and the licensing of data, in IT environments has evolved over the last couple of decades, and nowhere has this been more necessary and prolific than in GIS systems.

The reason for this is that GIS systems are data centric. That is, without good GIS (or spatial) data, much of the capability of a GIS system will not be realised. In this context, "good" data is data which is correct, complete, context sensitive, current and appropriate for the task at hand. Because data is expensive to collect and maintain, it is a valuable resource which is typically hard won and often collected at considerable cost.

Most GIS systems contain a lot of data which could be described as reference data, or "base data" onto which the user would add his or her data. An example of reference data would be the data commonly available on Google Maps or similar products. These "Public Domain" data sets have been collected for general use and are used on a wide range of applications. For example, when one orders a pizza online, it will generally include a maplet showing the location of the pizza store in relation to the user, and in some cases show the route of the delivery van, along with the GPS location of the van in real-time.

As such, Google Maps are extensively used and while Google's business model is such that they do not charge for the use of data, they do derive a significant business benefit in other ways, such as driving eyeballs to their site and the companies that use and advertise on their site.

Other data providers do not use the same business model and sell, or more correctly license, their data to end users. An example of this is Nearmap (refer Glossary Reference 13) who provide high quality and frequently updated aerial imagery using a licensing regime based on an annual / monthly subscription.

Other data licensing models can include Creative Commons (refer Glossary Reference 14) data licensing with a philosophy exemplified by "Open data is data that can be freely used, re-used and redistributed by anyone – subject only, at most, to the requirement to attribute and sharealike."

However, a recent concern is that the Australian Federal Government considered introducing new sovereignty rules for government data that would require certain datasets to be hosted in accredited data centres within Australia.

This issue resulted from the government opting to use Amazon Web Services (AWS) to host its COVIDSafe contact tracing app. While AWS is legally required to host the COVIDSafe data in Australia under the specific legislation enacted, the move sparked concerns that US law enforcement could access the data. Of particular concern is the United States' Clarifying Lawful Overseas Use of Data Act (the CLOUD Act), which will allow for "reciprocal" data access with Australia if a bilateral agreement is signed.

Nevertheless, regardless of how data is collected and used, it (the data) is considered to be a valued and valuable asset worth protecting.

But concern for protecting a company's data asset, particularly spatial data, is not a new concept.

Over the last couple of centuries, Cartographers and map makers have been known for putting deliberate but subtle errors on to their maps so that they can track competitive products which might look similar to their own, and consequently prove that they are a copy.

A good example of this concept were the street directory map books, prolific in the decades leading up to the turn of the century. Most of the companies producing these books (eg Melways) generally added their own set of mis-information (extra streets, laneways, descriptions, etc) sprinkled throughout their books so that they could identify whether a competitive company had simply copied their work or created it all themselves.

When they found that a competitor had copied their work (including the additional misinformation), this then became proof for legal action to stop the theft of their IP.

That is, IP in its many forms is a very important and valuable asset for many companies and individuals.

Because IP can be licensed, it is available to be used by others if they pay the price and abide by the licensor's terms and conditions. Therefore, the theft of IP reduces the value of the asset to the company which owns the IP (because it has been stolen and others are now using it), as well as reducing the ability of the company to further develop the data product because part of its income stream has been stolen.

In this manner, and as we move more and more towards an "information society", the continued theft of IP becomes a blight on society, potentially adversely impacting the intelligent use of technology for the advancement of business, government and society as a whole.

Therefore, for a major national industry Association which purports to value Intellectual Property (as stated on its web site) to allow its President to attempt to steal someone else's IP and then to blatantly sign a Statutory Declaration, witnessed by a JP, saying that he will use "… these (reports) in my discussions with external parties" is an obvious contradiction.

Further, this type of behaviour is unethical and unprofessional and should not be condoned by any legitimate and professional organisation.

6 - …and now it becomes Devious

In Chapter 4, the story was introduced about how Gary, the President of an industry Association, had used his position in that Association to request IP (reports) from Bill, an Association member, for Association business.

In an email an hour later Gary said he would use those reports in his own consulting business, in competition with Bill, the author of those reports.

This attempt by Gary to steal Bill's IP was met by Bill's repeated request for Gary to sign a Statutory Declaration saying that he had deleted the reports and that that he would not use Bill's work in his own consulting business.

But Gary refused to respond. Bill had tried to be polite, but it was obvious that Gary was being devious and ducking any attempt by Bill to make contact with him regarding his (Bill's) IP.

This showed Gary's intent to do wrong and to try to steal Bill's IP.

Finally, Bill had had enough. He had spoken to Mark, a lawyer he had used before and asked him to write to Gary and point out that he was playing with fire. "Gary needs to understand that there are consequences for him trying to steal my IP and use it for his own business" Bill said, "and he needs to acknowledge that this is my property and what he did was wrong and inappropriate".

Bill was incensed over Gary's refusal to agree not to use Bill's IP. But when Gary sent the altered Statutory Declaration to Bill, that just made the matter worse. Gary was now saying in his Statutory Declaration that he would continue to use Bill's work. It was worse than saying nothing. But it also appeared that Gary was being belligerent and trying to exacerbate the situation.

Bill's lawyers sent the letter. This was over a month after Gary had originally tried to steal Bill's work. The letter from Bill's lawyers repeated Bill's demands and enclosed a Statutory Declaration for Gary to sign.

Gary ignored this letter.

A week later, Bill sent an email to Gary saying that he intended to write to the CEO of the Association of which Gary was President outlining Gary's actions. Gary ignored this email.

By this time, it was clear that Gary was just ignoring everything hoping that it would all go away.

Bill decided that he should call Lynette who was working with Gary on a project to enquire whether he was in hospital or otherwise incapacitated and therefore unable to respond to email or correspondence from his lawyers.

"Yes, Gary is working on a project with me," said Lynette. "He's fine, not in hospital. Why, what's wrong", she said. So, Bill told Lynette the story. Lynette agreed that it was a devious thing to do and recounted the story of one of her clients who had tried to reverse engineer some software that they had sold to them to go in competition with Lynette's company.

"It's wrong and immoral and incredibly stupid" she said, "just the sort of thing that a government employee would do who didn't think too far ahead and had no experience with developing software and running a business".

A few days later, Lynette emailed Bill with a copy of the Statutory Declaration that she had received from Gary, but which had not been sent to Bill. However, the Statutory Declaration that Lynette attached to her email was the same as the one that Gary had originally sent to Bill, but now with a JP signature.

That is, Gary was still insisting that that the following paragraph was appropriate:

"Having seen the reports, <u>I will refer to these in my discussion with external parties</u>, and if required will ask the individuals to contact you should they need further information." A redacted copy of this Statutory Declaration is shown in the Appendix at Item 2.

Bill was furious and responded to Lynette saying that if Gary was honest and reputable, he would just sign the Statutory Declaration that he (Bill) had drafted. By signing a different Statutory Declaration with different wording, Gary was showing that he was just being dishonest.

That afternoon, Bill again sent an email to Gary further threatening legal action.

Finally, a week later Gary signed and sent the Statutory Declaration which had been provided by Bill's lawyer. A redacted copy of this second Statutory Declaration is shown in the Appendix at Item 3.

This was some 6 weeks after Gary had originally tried to steal Bill's work.

Whether it was because of stupidity or belligerence, Gary's obfuscation and duplicity about signing the Statutory Declaration that Bill had requested resulted in no gain for Gary and just showed that he was a devious person, intent on getting away with trying to steal Bill's IP.

One concession extracted from Gary was that he promised Bill that he would disclose all of this to the management of the Association. While Bill was dubious that this would occur, he gave him the benefit of the doubt and accepted his statement.

"So that's the end of it," said Bill. "Six weeks of effort and several hundred dollars of lawyer's fees to send two letters before Gary would do the right thing and sign the Statutory Declaration to promise that he wouldn't use my reports for his company. What a devious person".

"And to think that he represents the Association and that I once considered that he was a professional person" fumed Bill.

In an earlier Chapter, the discussion about the concepts of professionalism and ethics highlighted that:

- Professionalism is defined as "the conduct, aims, or qualities that characterise or mark a profession or a professional person" and
- Ethics is defined as "relating to moral principles or the branch of knowledge dealing with these".

For both of these definitions, Gary failed the test, and failed it dismally.

Not only did Gary try to steal Bill's work, but he delayed and prevaricated and changed the wording in the Statutory Declaration to suit his ongoing desire to continue to use Bill's work.

It was bad enough that Gary tried to steal Bill's IP in the first place, but then to go on and say that he would continue to use that IP just highlighted how deliberate and pre-planned Gary's actions were. When Gary changed the wording on the Statutory Declaration, he showed a deliberate intent to do wrong and try to steal Bill's IP and more critically, to continue this wrong-doing into the future.

Gary showed himself as being devious, dishonest, unprofessional, unethical and lacking any moral compass or principles.

Unfortunately, he was now working as a Consultant in the industry and providing advice to unsuspecting organisations such as those discussed in Chapter 3 under the heading of Duplicitous Consulting Companies.

7 - The Detail is in the Coverup

About 6 months after Gary tried to steal Bill's IP, Bill received an email from a market research company commissioned by the Association asking for "relevant research" about the IT industry for an upcoming Queensland conference. The fact that Bill received this request was a surprise given the angst which had occurred six months earlier when Gary tried to steal Bill's IP on the same topic.

This request was concerning to Bill because it highlighted:

- that perhaps Gary had not disclosed to the Association's management that he had tried to steal Bill's IP as he had promised, otherwise they would not have the temerity to ask Bill to provide information; and
- the Association was willing to commission (and obviously pay) a market research company to undertake research which was similar to the content in the reports undertaken by Bill's company which Gary had tried to steal.

Needless to say, Bill did not provide any information.

A year later, Bill received another email from the NSW Manager of the Association saying:

"The Association is wanting to complete our own industry survey. As part of your company's 2018 survey did you ask questions which would be relevant and if so, could you please send me your data".

Bill was aghast – they were at it again.

As if it was not bad enough that they tried to steal his work 18 months earlier, they were now asking him to give them all his research – for free. Obviously, the work undertaken by the market research company commissioned the year earlier resulted in nothing useful so now they were trying to do the "good cop" routine to get Bill's data.

Bill was lost for words. The Association clearly had not learnt a thing from the events of the previous year.

This was the catalyst that turned Bill's anger to fury.

Up until that point he did not want to embarrass the Association by lodging a complaint against their President. After all, Bill had been a Director of the Association in the past and had spent some considerable time and effort running committees and managing conferences and seminars for the Association. The last thing he wanted to do was to start a process which might reflect badly on the Association.

But enough was enough!

So, Bill responded to the NSW manager of the Association with an outline of Gary's attempt to steal his IP some 18 months previously, attaching copies of key emails and letters from Bill's lawyers to Gary.

The NSW manager of the Association forwarded his email to Peter, the CEO of the Association who did nothing – just ignored everything.

Clearly, the Association had not learnt from the previous debacle and had not tried to fix their management processes, so in frustration Bill emailed Peter the CEO directly outlining the events of Gary's attempt to steal his IP and the subsequent attempts by Gary to re-write the Statutory Declaration so that it would favour Gary's attempt to continue to use Bill's IP.

Bill's email stated that Gary, their (then) President, had promised to bring this issue to the attention of the Association's senior management but it was clear from the recent correspondence with the Association that Gary had not done so.

The Association's CEO responded by suggesting Bill was making all of this up, despite the emails from Gary (which Bill provided) showing that this was not the case. But he did say that Bill would have to make it into a formal complaint which Peter would send to the Professional Standards Committee for investigation.

Bill was sceptical and thought that this would not achieve anything and just be whitewashed, so he requested that if this route were followed, that an independent observer be on the Professional Standards Committee to ensure that it was a fair and independent investigation. This was refused – it was clear that they were not going to have any oversight to processes which might show that such processes were lacking.

Now the first stage of any cover-up is to "duck and weave", much like on a football field where the player with the ball is trying to get through the backs to score. The first stage of "ducking and weaving" is to palm it off to a committee for investigation. While Bill knew this would likely happen and that it was probably the most appropriate action to take, the cynic in him thought that this was just the start of a delaying "do nothing" process.

The smart thing to do when faced with evidence of malfeasance would be to "fess up" and take a small hit, accept that you have been caught out, maybe make a small apology, minimise the damage and then move on.

But the marketing person's dogma is usually to "deny, deny, deny" and keep doing so until everything goes away.

While Bill thought that there was some hope that he would get a fair process, he was doubtful that this would be the case. The Association had already settled into the "deny, deny, deny" pattern and were starting to position themselves to block any further discussion.

By this stage Bill had provided a large amount of correspondence including emails as evidence supporting his claims, but in truth the

Association were not going to follow an honest and ethical path in order to resolve this issue. They were in the "deny, deny, deny" mode and they were not going to change.

Then they started the next stage – to discredit Bill for lodging the complaint. That is, "shoot the whistle-blower" and try to discredit him which, of course, further infuriated Bill.

So, the events at that time could be summarised as follows:

1. Bill emailed Peter the Association's CEO outlining the issue of Gary attempting to steal his IP and attached numerous emails to support his facts. Bill said that he did not intend to lodge a formal complaint but was forced to when Peter said that this was the only process that could be followed and if a formal complaint was not lodged, then the matter would be closed.

2. While Bill was pondering the most appropriate response to this, Peter the CEO said that he would refer Bill's material to the complaints committee without Bill's approval and in so doing would make it into a formal complaint. Bill was not sure if this was just a "try on" to get Bill to backdown and withdraw his suggestion of a complaint, such as it was at that stage, or whether this was a serious escalation of the process.

However, 8 days later Peter the CEO said that he could not refer Bill's material to the committee without Bill's approval and if Bill did not agree then he would consider the matter closed. This was a very provocative statement to make and one which would likely not be conducive to any reasonable outcome.

This statement showed that Peter had changed the rules from:

- saying he would refer Bill's documents to the committee without Bill's approval; to
- saying that he could not refer Bill's documents to the committee without Bill's approval.

That is, there was a 180-degree reversal of the previous direction that was made over an 8-day period. This highlighted to Bill that Peter the CEO of the Association was "making up policy on the run" and changing that policy to suit their purposes as they saw fit.

3. Bill initially wanted to have a conversation about Gary's actions before considering whether to take it to a formal complaint, but because of the outright refusal by the Association CEO to consider anything other than a formal complaint, Bill made the decision to lodge this issue as a formal complaint with the Association.

4. Bill received the Notice of Receipt of Complaint from Peter the CEO a week later.

In any organisation, the lodging of a formal complaint about a member of the executive, or a senior staff person, is fraught with difficulties. To avoid a "Caesar judging Caesar" situation, it is normal (and very healthy) for the organisation to have a formal complaints investigation committee and process to do all the investigations and to report back to senior management of the organisation in due course.

This complaints committee is normally held at "arm's length" from the organisation itself, so that there is not only a degree of independence, but that it is also seen to be independent.

The Association appointed James from Adelaide to the role of Chair of the Complaints Committee to run the investigation. Bill was impressed with this decision because James had a reputation as being an honest "straight-shooter" who was fair and independent.

"All I want is a fair and honest investigation", said Bill. "I don't want a cover-up and I don't want a show trial. I just want this issue to be properly and professionally looked at and a decision made to the satisfaction of all parties over the long term."

However, as events unfolded over the next few weeks and months, it appeared that this was not going to be a fair investigation, and certainly not an honest investigation. It was clear that James was really just trying to make the complaint go away and in so doing, to discredit Bill.

All Associations have (or should have) a Constitution and / or Articles of Association. This industry Association had a Constitution and Clause 3.3 of the Association's Complaints and Disciplinary Rules stated that "within 20 business days of Notice of Receipt of Complaint ... the Chair shall (a) reject the complaint or (b) refer the complaint to informal mediation or (c) refer the complaint to the complaints committee for investigation"

5. Bill did not hear from James until almost 2 months later, when James wrote to Bill saying that he had made an initial determination and he would refer the complaint to the Complaints Committee for Investigation.

Given that the Association had formally acknowledged receipt of the complaint two months earlier and that the Association's own rules allowed 20 business days to respond, this notice from James was almost a month outside of the 20 business days to respond, even allowing for the Christmas break. This was pointed out to James who dismissed any concerns and said that rule did not apply.

6. James then went on to provide Bill's complaint to Gary even though the complaint procedure did NOT make provisions for the respondent (that is, Gary) to read and comment on Bill's complaint. James said that the respondent was given 28 days to read and provide comment, even though this was not in the Association's own complaint procedure.

So, even though Gary was given a copy of Bill's complaint, Bill did not receive a copy of Gary's comments, which procedural fairness would suggest should occur. Again, this was raised with James who dismissed Bill's concern and yet again said that rule also did not apply. These rules were documented in the Complaints procedure documentation on the Association's web site so when James changed the rules it was evident for all to see.

Some 7 months after the complaint was lodged, James emailed Bill saying that Gary had provided his response 2 weeks earlier, some 3½ months after the due date of 28 days from James original letter in point 5 above. Again, this was raised with James who dismissed Bill's concern and yet again changed the rules. Gary was not censured by James for ignoring the rules and providing his response over 3½ months late.

This process showed that not only did the Association not follow their own rules, but that preferential treatment was being given to one side (Gary) over the other (Bill). James was quick to point out that Bill needed to respond to any correspondence within certain timeframes, but when it came for Gary to respond, or for James to respond in a prompt manner to letters from Bill's lawyers, the timeframes were ignored.

"There are one set of rules for them, and one for me", said Bill "I'm becoming more and more concerned that this is all just a set-up to lead to a pre-determined outcome, which won't be in my favour".

Nevertheless, Bill persisted. By this time he had enlisted the support of lawyers to try and make sure that his interests were being served as well as to make it obvious to James and the Association that this was serious and that he was not just going to go away.

7. In the same email from James that he (James) said that he would refer it to the Complaints Committee, it was obvious (through an email mix-up where Bill was incorrectly copied into an email chain) that there was not any complaints committee and that one would have to be formed.

8. Nevertheless, a month later, James wrote to say "…the Complaints Committee and the Investigating Committee propose to appoint a Retired Judge to hear and determine the complaint". So, over a period of 3 weeks, there were now two committees involved – the Complaints Committee and the Investigation Committee. Again, this was not in accordance with Association's own rules and when

Bill's lawyers pointed this out to James, he dismissed this concern and yet again changed the rules.

By this stage, it was becoming abundantly clear to Bill that James was changing the Association's own rules, and making up new rules, whenever he felt like doing so. Apart from being unfair and not appropriate, it was also not in keeping with any rules of probity.

Good probity depends on:

- making a plan for how a process is run (whether that process is an investigation of a complaint or an investigation of a tender);
- getting the plan agreed and signed-off by all parties and management; and then
- proceeding with the agreed plan.

Changing the rules of an investigation after the investigation had stated was certainly not in keeping with basic probity concepts, as well as not being fair and not being conducive to a good outcome.

An analogy would be to change the rules of a football game after the game had started.

Picture the following scenario:

Two teams are playing a hard and evenly matched game of football surrounded by a sell-out crowd of cheering fans. The referee suddenly decides to award a free kick to one team because he decided that the 10-yard rule really should be 15-yards. So, the player that was at 12-yards was penalised and a free kick taken against him. A player from the opposing team takes the free kick and goes on to score a goal.

How do you think would that play out at the game with 50,000 spectators? Would it be fair to say that the referee himself would be given a free kick to the side-lines so that another more competent referee could take over? I think everyone would agree with that likely scenario.

But not in the Association. James, the Chair of the Investigation Committee (that is, the referee) arbitrarily decided that the written rules in the Association's own documentation could be ignored and that he could re-write the rules during the investigation process as it suited him. He did this not just once, he did it at least 5 times. He was not censured by the current President of the Association, despite Bill's lawyers writing to the President on multiple occasions pointing this out.

9. Following on from James' email saying that a Retired Judge would be appointed to determine the complaint, James' Solicitor emailed 3 weeks later that the Judge had indeed been appointed. The Judge had written a "Complaint Determination Deed" which James' Solicitor attached for Bill to sign.

A Deed such as this is quite common in matters of this type and is, in effect, an agreement outlining the issues to be decided. The Deed requires all parties to sign which signals their agreement with the content of the Deed and to proceed.

8 - Can you trust a Retired Judge?

Although Bill had some reservations about signing the "Complaint Determination Deed" from the Retired Judge, he did so on the expectation that a person of the stature of a Judge (retired or not) in charge of the process would ensure that the process was proper and correct, and that it really would be independent.

It was also obvious from the correspondence that the Retired Judge was in Adelaide along with James and James' Solicitor. So, while Bill thought that this was "a bit too cosy for comfort", he reminded himself that this was a "Retired Judge" after all, and a person who was (by nature of the beast) independent and above taking sides one way or another.

Therefore, Bill steeled himself to commit to the process and duly signed the Deed in the expectation that a proper process would be followed.

10. Then several weeks later the Retired Judge sent a letter to all parties, referring to the Complaints Determination Deed and said in Clause 2.1.3 of that letter "...I note from a perusal of the papers, that most of the background circumstances are not contested."

This was an exceptional statement for the Retired Judge to make, given that there was no agreement on the background circumstances, and indeed the background circumstances were the crux of the complaint.

The Retired Judge later tried to back off this statement and said his words were "taken out of context". Therefore, in order to provide a factual record of this issue, an extract from the letter from the Retired Judge is shown below (refer also Appendix Item 4), which said after a bit of preamble:

"I propose the following program:

"2.   Preliminary Hearing

"First, I suggest that there be a Preliminary Hearing between the Parties, their representatives and myself, in which there will be an informal discussion of the Procedure to be followed and its timing. The following matters need to be discussed.

"2.1   Particulars of Misconduct and Response

"2.1.1   I direct that the complainant be prepared to participate and characterise the conduct which he claims was breached by both Respondents (that is, Gary and the Association). In other words the Complainant needs to assert that the conduct amounted to a breach of a particular clause in the Governing Documents. Further, the Complainant should identify what penalty he seeks (n.b. the possible penalties are outlined in Clause 8.3 of the Constitution).

"2.1.2   So too I direct the two respondents (Gary and the Association) to articulate a response to the Complaint as particularised. Some time may be necessary for this to happen. I will detail a timeline for the provision of such particulars and the response hereto.

"2.1.3   Further to this, I note from a perusal of the papers that most of the background circumstances are not contested. For example the fact of the request for the reports and the confrontation that followed appear to be agreed and perhaps the parties could give consideration to their being an agreed factual background."

Again, the comments in Clause 2.1.3 (above) of the letter from the Retired Judge were extraordinary.

Bill had not been provided with any of Gary's comments on his complaint, despite requesting these from James on several occasions, so he (Bill) could not understand how the Retired Judge could make such a statement, unless Gary had agreed with Bill's complaint, which was highly unlikely. Bill regarded that the role of the Retired Judge was to investigate and adjudicate the complaint, not to dismiss it as "not contested".

Further, the Retired Judge's statement in the same Clause that "the request for the reports and the confrontation that followed appear to be agreed" was just not true.

"Yes", Bill said "the request for the reports was partially correct in that the reports were requested by Gary the President of the Association and provided to Gary as the Association's representative, not to Gary the consultant which Gary attested to in his Statutory Declaration a few weeks later. Similarly, the confrontation that followed was also not agreed. Gary had refused to sign the Statutory Declaration that Bill's lawyer had prepared and had instead substituted his own that said he was going to continue to use Bill's work. That is, Gary said in his Statutory Declaration that he intended to continue to use Bill's IP."

This letter also highlighted that the Retired Judge's office had the same address as James' Solicitor and that the email address of the Retired Judge was also the same as James' Solicitor.

So how could the Retired Judge be independent when he was sharing the same offices with James' lawyer and had, no doubt, had conversations with James and his lawyer which he did not have with the other parties.

That is, just 13 days after Bill signed the Complaint Determination Deed to commence arbitration, and before arbitration commenced, the Retired Judge said that the "… circumstances are not contested", and he did this while working from the offices of James' Solicitor. Extraordinary!

Obviously, Bill had every right to think that this was "a bit too cosy for comfort" and a bit "too inbred".

Independence, by definition, requires some distance from all parties and in a situation where some of the parties are working in close quarters, it could be argued that the veil of independence could easily break down, as it had appeared to be doing in these circumstances.

11. A week later Bill's lawyers therefore requested the documentation from the Retired Judge with which he had made the determination that "... *most of the background circumstances are not contested"*. That information was not provided. Bill's lawyers also requested a number of documents from Gary and the Association. These documents were also not provided.

12. At the same time, Bill's lawyers also sent a letter to James requesting mediation, given that the Association complaints investigation process was based on mediation, not arbitration and by now Bill was reluctant to enter into Arbitration given the Retired Judge's comments which indicated that he was not independent.

13. A month later, James agreed to mediation. In that letter James stated that "Gary has not provided a response to the Complaint but will be asked to do so in preparation for the mediation".

Bill was now very confused.

If James' statement that Gary had not provided a response was correct, then how could the Retired Judge come to the statement in his letter several months previously that "...the background circumstances are not contested". Unless he was clairvoyant, or unless James had told the Retired Judge a version of events which then led the Retired Judge to say that the "... circumstances are not contested".

Was someone misleading and confusing everything? It could not be the Retired Judge – after all, he should be above this type of misdirection?

14. A month later Bill's lawyers yet again wrote to James asking when they could expect the documents that had been requested two months previously. Bill's lawyers again referred to the email from James at the start of this process where he said that "... Gary is given 28 days to respond from the formal notification by Peter the CEO of the complaint". This said that Gary had been asked to respond and since the Retired Judge had said the "... background circumstances were not in contention", then it seemed that Gary's response had in fact been provided to James.

It was becoming more and more obvious that someone was playing a bit "fast and loose" with the truth. If it was not the Retired Judge, then it had to be James, because Gary did not seem to be a part of many of these conversations.

15. So, after the request for mediation, James emailed that a month earlier he had asked the Association to provide information and documents relevant to the complaint but these documents had not (as at that date) been provided. James also confirmed that Gary had not provided a response to the complaint as that date and that all documents provided to the Retired Judge had been provided to Bill's lawyers. James attached the statement from Gary which had been received two weeks prior which was 3½ months late given that it was to have been produced (according to James' earlier edict) within 28 days of the initial request. Gary was 3½ months late, but he was not censured for this delay. James dismissed Bill's concern for yet another change of the rules.

This was becoming murkier and murkier. How could the Retired Judge say the background circumstances were not contested when he supposedly had not received any information from Gary. Was the Retired Judge lying (hard to accept) or was James lying (more likely)?

By this time, Bill had formed the opinion that James had probably had several conversations with the Retired Judge and also had several conversations with Gary. It appeared that James may have briefed the Retired Judge, based on these conversations. While the

Retired Judge may have naively believed James' commentary as the truth, it was heavily jaundiced.

Nevertheless, the statement by the Retired Judge made it very clear that he was not independent.

16. A month later Bill's lawyers yet again wrote to the Retired Judge requesting the documentation that had caused him to come to the statement he made in his letter that the "… circumstances were not in contention". No response was received from the Retired Judge, and in fact no response has ever been received from the Retired Judge. Again, James dismissed Bill's concern for this blatant omission as not being relevant.

17. At this time, Bill's lawyers also wrote to Faz, the current President of the Association in an attempt to expedite the release of documentation which appeared to be being held by the Retired Judge and the Association and not being provided. In that letter, Bill's lawyers pointed out that the Association Complaint and Disciplinary Rules (Clause 6.2.3) provide that "… the Investigating Committee treat the Complainant with respect, fairness and in accordance with the rules of natural justice." Since this had not happened, Bill's lawyers invited Faz, the President of Association to consider the performance of James in his role as Chair of this complaints process. Faz did not respond to this letter.

18. In a further letter to Faz from James a month later, James said that "I confirm that at the time that the Retired Judge prepared and delivered his letter, neither Gary nor the Association had responded to the complaint".

Therefore, one would seriously have to question how the Retired Judge could come to such an astounding conclusion that the "… circumstances were not in contention" when he had not at that time (according to the letter from James) received any documentation to make such a determination.

19. In a further letter from James to Faz on the same date, James stated "The Association has not provided a response to the Complaint. I will ask the Association to prepare a response in the form of a position paper prior to mediation". That position paper response was not provided. Faz did not respond to this letter.

By this time, it was obvious to Bill that the continuing theme from the Association and James was that of delaying and obfuscation. "They either don't respond to letters from my lawyers, or they say that they will do something and then don't do it. It's like dealing with a marshmallow – you hit one side and your hand just disappears and then when you take it out, there's no mark where your hand once was."

This highlighted that a clear and unfortunate pattern had developed:

- the Association and the Complaints Chair agreed to a process, such as to have a professional investigation to the complaint and finalise an outcome, and
- then they set about to either destroy or to compromise that process.

Bill was becoming frustrated, not only because of the very lengthy delay and endless manipulations by James and the Association, but also because it was costing some substantial amount of money for his lawyers which so far had achieved very little.

Bill thought that James had demonstrated that his mission in life was to delay, deny, ignore and misdirect until Bill either ran out of money for lawyers, or grew old and died. He thought that Faz was not much different, because he was ignoring everything and leaving it up to James.

"This is just a cycle that is on repeat, and nobody in the Association appears to be interested or concerned about what is happening" said Bill.

That is, it was very obvious by this stage that the Association had no clear management process and no one accountable to complete any task.

All of these issues demonstrated that there was a lack of governance from the Association as well as from James and Faz with, in some cases, this being extreme.

It was also abundantly clear that there was no governance around the investigation process, no governance around the Arbitration / Mediation process and no governance to guide the correspondence with James and Faz, the latter providing no response to any correspondence at all.

There was certainly no governance around the issue of James hiring the Retired Judge to arbitrate when that process was not allowed under the Association rules. There was no governance around the utterances from the Retired Judge, resulting in the Retired Judge discrediting himself as partisan.

Good governance involves having good processes and having those processes documented. This documentation should describe the processes and that which needs to occur at different milestones in these processes.

Having good processes involves having good management of those processes. In all instances, the actions of the Association and its representatives (particularly James and Faz) showed that there was no management of the processes and that the processes were being "made up on the run".

The outcome of this lack of management control of processes, lack of documentation response and lack of governance resulted in a shambolic approach to all components of the investigation, mediation and outcome with James and Faz clearly showing a very high level of incompetence.

The Board collectively and Directors individually also exhibited a lack of governance, lack of interest and lack of control of the events surrounding the investigation of the complaint.

9 - Arbitration v Mediation – what's the difference?

The Complaint Determination Deed sent by the Retired Judge had dictated that the process would be based on Arbitration.

The rules of the Association as outlined in its Constitution and Complaints procedure mandated that any complaints process must be based on Mediation.

These two processes are quite different and can have a significantly different outcome for participants. In order to understand the issues involved, it may be useful to take a step back and look at the two processes:

Arbitration:

The Australian Disputes Centre defines Arbitration (refer Glossary Reference 15) as "…a process in which the parties to a dispute present arguments and evidence to a dispute resolution practitioner (the arbitrator) who makes a determination. The process is private and, subject to the parties' agreement, can be confidential. Arbitration offers a flexible and efficient means of resolving disputes both domestically and internationally. The decision of the arbitral tribunal is final and binding. The award is enforceable."

In effect, Arbitration is a court process with the Arbitrator sitting in judgement on the parties who argue their case. Because the court system in Australia is confrontational, arguments can often be put forcefully from one side to the other.

In this confrontational court-room style, it is not uncommon for Barristers to use a line of questioning that can become intimidating and antagonistic. This type of confrontational style is designed to "break down" one of the parties in the hope that they may then contradict their story.

"The aim of the opposing Barrister is to make you get angry", said a top silk (Barrister) during a lengthy court case recently. "And when you get angry, you often say things that you would not otherwise say. You really need to keep your cool, stay calm and answer the questions with as much calm as possible. Just ignore his intimidation and keep cool".

Unfortunately, often the result of arbitration processes of this type is that it is not conducive to an outcome on which all sides agree. It is usually only of benefit to the side with the most skilled (and therefore often the most expensive) legal team winning at the expense of the side which does not have the resources to fight a very expensive fight.

As such, this process benefits the larger party with the deepest pockets, and in the case of the Association versus Bill, Arbitration would always favour the Association, because the Association could field the best and most expensive team of lawyers and Barristers. After all, the Financial Statements from the most recent AGM showed that the Association had over a million dollars of assets and several hundred thousand dollars in liquid funds in various bank accounts and investments.

Mediation:

Mediation, on the other hand, is a very different process.

The Australian Disputes Centre defines Mediation (refer Glossary Reference 16) as "… a process in which the parties to a dispute, with the assistance of a dispute resolution practitioner (the mediator), identify the disputed issues, develop options, consider alternatives and endeavour to reach an agreement. The mediator has no advisory or determinative role in regard to the content of the dispute or the outcome of its resolution but may advise on or determine the process of mediation whereby resolution is attempted. Mediation may be undertaken voluntarily, under a court order, or subject to an existing contractual agreement."

Mediation can be a dynamic, structured, interactive process where an impartial third-party assists in resolving the conflict through the use of specialised communication and negotiation techniques.

That is, Mediation is an attempt to arrive at a reasoned compromise between the parties after each side provides their evidence and grievances. The key here is compromise, which means that each side will likely "give ground" to come to an outcome which is agreed by all parties. No strong language, no intimidation, no expensive lawyers – just reasoned discussion and compromise.

In the context of this complaint, the difference between Mediation and Arbitration is that:

- the outcome of Mediation is conciliation, based on agreement between the parties; whereas
- the outcome of Arbitration is based on a Judge's decision, which may not be agreed by one or both parties.

That is, Mediation comes to a joint agreement, whereas Arbitration is based on the parties being told the outcome, whether they like it or not and whether there is any agreement on that outcome by either, or both parties.

Importantly:

- Arbitration is not subject to appeal – the Judge's decision is final, but Mediation usually continues until agreement is reached between both parties.
- Arbitration is not able to award costs, whereas Mediation can include a costs apportionment.

That is, with a compliant Judge, Arbitration becomes a very effective method to "railroad the process" to achieve an outcome which is pre-determined. So because there is no possibility of appeal, the parties "get what they are told", regardless of whether it is fair or agreed.

That is, to stress the key difference:

- Mediation arrives at a joint agreement, whereas
- Arbitration results in the parties being told the outcome, whether there is any agreement on that outcome by either or both parties.

Because the Complaint Determination Deed as drafted by the Retired Judge and sent to James as the format for moving forward was based on Arbitration, not Mediation, it was a "loose hand-grenade" which would likely explode when ready, particularly given that the Retired Judge had appeared to have already made up his mind on specific issues in a fact-free environment.

So, while Bill was initially concerned that the process outlined in the Complaint Determination Deed was based on Arbitration, rather than Mediation, when the Retired Judge sent his letter several weeks later saying that the "circumstances were not contested", Bill became even more concerned.

"This is obviously a set-up." he said. "They have proposed Arbitration so that they can hand down a verdict, which will be that I'm just making all this up and then use that to discredit me. But they have shown their hand with the follow-up letter."

Bill made it clear that he was not going to proceed with Arbitration after the Retired Judge had already said that he had made up his mind without having received all statements and documentation, nor without having spoken to the witness.

10 - It is agreed upon...

Finally! James had agreed to Mediation rather than Arbitration.

While he did not admit it, it seemed that the series of letters and emails from Bill's lawyers to James and Faz had the desired effect. James now seemed to understand that Bill's lawyers would not accept an Arbitrated process, particularly when the Retired Judge had declared, through his own letter, that he was not impartial, and that neither the Retired Judge, James nor Faz would respond to any requests as to how he came to such an astounding conclusion before any facts were presented.

Accordingly, Bill's lawyers and James' lawyers arranged for the Mediation process to be actioned. An independent Mediator was selected who had the software and processes in place for the mediation to be undertaken on-line. This was important given that James and his lawyer were based in Adelaide, Faz was based in Melbourne and Gary and Bill were based in Sydney, albeit that neither Gary nor Bill would ever be likely to share a meeting room together by this time.

The online Mediation process was more complex than just a simple video conference, given that separate "rooms" or sub-meeting environments were available for the process as well as several other features necessary to ensure a confidential but transparent process was undertaken. The Mediation software was loaded on each of the desktops of the parties in the days leading up to the Mediation and each party was required to view a short training course before commencement.

20. Mediation was undertaken a month after James had agreed to follow the process as outlined in the Associations' own rules. However, the Mediation comprised of Gary, James and his Solicitor, Bill and his lawyers and Michael from Hobart. Faz, the Association

President, was the nominated Association representative and Board member but did not appear, so Michael from Hobart attended in the place of Faz. Michael stated that he was NOT a Board member and therefore did NOT have the authority to make a decision at the mediation.

Michael's presence in the Mediation raised several issues:

- Firstly, Michael was a late-comer to the Mediation process and had not pre-loaded the software nor undertaken the video training course, so the first 40 minutes of the Mediation was wasted in getting Michael online and up to speed with the process.
- Secondly, Michael said that he was not a Board member of the Association and could therefore not make a decision. He said that he was only a member of the Association so all he could do would be to take a "preferred decision" back to the Board for their agreement. As such, because there was no decision maker from the Association at the Mediation, this largely invalidated the mediation process.

The objective of any Mediation is to Mediate (as obvious as that sounds).

That is, a Mediation is for all parties to arrive at an agreed outcome and that could not happen if one of the parties could not agree to an outcome nor make a decision.

So, it was clear that the actions of Faz had effectively sabotaged the mediation. By Faz not bothering to attend the Mediation, the result was that the complaint was not able to be progressed and therefore nothing was achieved.

Bill said that the only outcome was that he wasted several thousand dollars paying for two lawyers to attend a Mediation that was doomed from the start.

21. However, during the mediation, Michael made the astounding statement that:

- he was new to this complaint and had not read the background material; but
- he had investigated the complaint; and
- found that there was no case to answer.

This was simply an astounding statement to make.

In his real job, Michael was a Departmental head of a major State Government agency in Hobart, so as a senior bureaucrat, one would assume that he had a modicum of intelligence and would have known the processes which are used in day-to-day business activities.

To make such a statement which was contradictory, fact-free and baseless was just stunning. Bill said that everyone was sitting there stunned for the next few minutes. "He even surprised his own side with such an outrageous statement", said Bill.

This statement by Michael was an obvious attempt to "whitewash" the complaint based on no information and no evidence and without speaking with the parties.

It was also very noticeable that James did not contradict Michael. James sat there on his video feed; mouth open with surprise but he did not contradict Michael. He just let the statement rest, thereby condoning the whitewashing of Bill's complaint by Michael.

22. In the week following the aborted mediation attempt, Bill's lawyers wrote to Faz about a number of issues which occurred during the mediation, including:

- the Association not having an authorised representative in attendance at the mediation and therefore voiding the mediation;
- the Association failing to inform the mediation company that Faz would not be attending and therefore wasting considerable time of the mediator having to make alternative arrangements;
- the Association failing to consider any compromise; and

- the Association attempting to whitewash the complaint and the complaints process.

Faz did not bother to respond to this letter.

23. That is, the Association had not attended the Mediation in good faith with an authorised representative and did not make any offer of compromise.

24. It was apparent that the Association had deliberately undermined the mediation.

25. Bill's lawyers also wrote to James referring to previous unanswered letters and requests for documentation from the Retired Judge and the Association, highlighting again that this information remained to be provided. The requested information had not been provided by the Association or from the Retired Judge despite Bill's lawyers repeatedly asking for it. James ignored this letter from Bill's lawyers.

By this time, it was obvious that the whole process was a farce and that the Association had no intention of investigating or rationally dealing with the complaint.

During this time, no statements had been requested from Lynette, the only person who was a witness to the events. Lynette could have told James about her discussions with Bill and with Gary and her part in trying to get Gary to respond to Bill's emails and to get Gary to not use Bill's IP illegally.

Nevertheless, by this time it became reasonably apparent that the Association was a fumbling and bumbling organisation which had no management processes of any consequence, and certainly no processes to deal with a complaint. It clearly had no grasp of process, probity, professionalism or ethics.

Despite the Association being well known in the GIS industry and despite having produced a number of booklets and web pages dedicated to their (supposed) professional approach, when the chips were down and they had to "walk the walk" rather than just "talk the talk" they were found severely wanting.

It also became obvious that Bill's complaint was probably the first and only complaint ever made, so they had no history of dealing with complaints and therefore no corporate knowledge of these types of processes, particularly given the ongoing change of Directors did not engender any retention of corporate knowledge. This then had led Directors and management to "reinvent the wheel" on a number of issues.

But it was also clear that the failings of the Association in the progression of this complaint were many and that they occurred on many different levels.

a) The Association showed that they were not taking Bill's complaint seriously, as shown by the Association obviously not reading the email exchanges which contradicted Gary's later "statement" that the theft of Bill's IP "didn't happen", as well as by not requesting a statement from the only witness, Lynette.

b) The Association did not follow any sort of due process and changed their own rules on a number of occasions while admonishing Bill if he failed to meet their rules. This happened on such a large number of times that it was clear that they were "making it up as they went along".

c) The Association appointed James to Chair the "Complaints Investigation Committee", who did not investigate the complaint and sought only to frustrate any attempt to resolve this issue.

d) James sought to add a veneer of judicial process over the top by retaining the Retired Judge in a feeble attempt of a "show trial" later becoming obvious when the Retired Judge disqualified himself by his statement that the "… circumstances were not in contention", when in fact that was the basis of the complaint.

e) James continued to insist that an arbitration process should be followed when the Association's own rules stated that mediation was the only process that should be followed.

f) James continued to insist that arbitration must be undertaken by the Retired Judge who (by that time) had discredited himself and shown that he was not independent.

g) Faz the Association President continued to support James and did not attend mediation or provide a replacement who could make a decision, thereby voiding the mediation.

h) Michael, Faz's mediation replacement who could not make a decision, then attempted to blatantly and childishly whitewash the complaint with James' support.

But the crux of the ineptitude of the Association was the appointment of the Retired Judge by James and his statement that the "… circumstances were not in contention" in his letter. The only way that he could make this statement was because he had been told to say this by James, the Chair of the Investigation Committee.

26. Unbelievably, over a month after the failed Mediation attempt, the Solicitor acting for James wrote to Bill's lawyers again pursuing the use of Retired Judge for arbitration. This was despite the Retired Judge's independence having been discredited by this time since he was unable and unwilling to provide any documentation or reason as to how he had arrived at the statement that the. "… circumstances were not in contention" in his letter when it was then apparent that he had not received any documentation at that time to make such a determination.

27. Further letters from Bill's lawyers to James again said that despite having signed a deed, that Bill would not be participating in an arbitration where the conclusion was already foregone as stated by the Retired Judge in his letter that the "… circumstances were not in contention" when he had not received any documentation to make such a determination.

Certainly, if the correspondence from James was to be believed, Gary did not provide his submission until two months after the letter from the Retired Judge, so therefore the information did not come from Gary's submission.

It was clear that someone was not telling the truth. Either:

- the Retired Judge was a clairvoyant (not likely) and knew what Gary was going to write some 2 months later; or
- James had told the Retired Judge a story which the Retired Judge believed without checking and which then became the basis of his damming statement (more likely); or
- either or both of these two individuals were lying (quite probable).

Either way, there was no way that Bill was going to agree to a process to resolve the complaint as outlined in James's Complaints Determination Deed when the Retired Judge who was going to judge that complaint said in a letter 2 weeks after the Determination Deed was signed, that "… the background circumstances are not contested." The judge had already reached a foregone conclusion even before Gary had lodged his response to the complaint some 2 months later.

So, either James was lying, or the Retired Judge was lying.

Bill said that he knew a set-up when he saw it. It was obvious that James has set this up to whitewash Gary and the Association and make out that Bill was a trouble-maker.

11 - Tracking the Footprints

Initially all that Bill had wanted from lodging the complaint with the Association was recognition from the Association that Gary's actions in trying to steal Bill's IP were wrong, and perhaps an apology.

As the events progressed and became more vitriolic and expensive, Bill would have settled for reimbursement of his legal fees and an apology. Indeed, his closing letter to the Board said that he was not seeking damages at that stage, but only reimbursement of his expenses.

However, the intransigence of James, Faz and the Association to not progress his complaint at even the most basic level of professional competence hardened Bill's resolve to seek a public apology with an admission of wrong doing from both Gary and the Association.

By this time, Bill was convinced that the "investigation" of the complaint was, at best superficial and at worst, not occurring at all.

It was also obvious that nothing was going to come out of the "investigation". The decision to "deny, deny, deny" had already been made and was now fully operational in the Association's strategy.

By this time, Gary had provided his response to Bill's complaint with words along the lines of "it didn't happen", "we had a number of follow-up phone calls and Bill had agreed that he had over-reacted", etc, etc. So, Gary's argument was that it was all a misunderstanding by Bill – putting the blame solely on Bill.

According to Gary, he had done the right thing and Bill had got it all wrong. To accept this proposition, one would have to ignore all the written evidence of emails and the Statutory Declaration from Gary that had said he was going to use Bill's IP and letters from Bill's lawyers. That is, Gary's premise was to ignore all the evidence and believe the smokescreen.

Even a superficial read of the evidence would show that Gary's argument fell apart very easily:

- If Gary's account was correct, then why were there a number of emails from both Bill and Gary which said the opposite? Even a cursory perusal of the email chain would show that something was amiss with Gary's account of the facts.
- If Gary's account was correct, then why would he (Gary) produce an alternative Statutory Declaration saying that he intended to continue using Bill's IP, and have that Statutory Declaration signed by a JP? He would not have done this if it had been a misunderstanding.
- If Gary's account was correct, then why would he (Gary) sign a second Statutory Declaration which supported the basis of Bill's complaint? He would not have done this if it had been a misunderstanding.
- If Gary's account was correct, then he could easily have produced phone records which showed that several calls were made by Gary to Bill's mobile in the stated time-frame. Even a feigned excuse that he had "lost the phone bill" is easily taken care of as the details of all calls are available from the provider, since legislation now requires telecommunications companies to retain metadata for several years and the metadata would have shown details (number called, time/date, duration of call, etc) of the calls placed. Of course, these phone bills were never produced because these would have shown that Gary did not make any calls to Bill as his statement suggested.
- If Gary's account was correct, then it would have conflicted with Lynette's emails and her later statement which also attested to the opposite.

Obviously the "investigation committee" run by James did not request any phone records from Gary because he was not interested in investigating the complaint.

In addition, and perhaps the most telling part of James's incompetence in investigating this complaint was that James never spoke to or requested a statement from Lynette, the witness to the theft of the IP.

Lynette ran her own software development company in Melbourne and was a Director of another (sister) industry Association to the one in question and was very well known in the industry and very credible.

Bill and Lynette had several verbal and email conversations just after Gary tried to steal Bill's IP about Gary's refusal to sign the Statutory Declaration that Bill had requested. Lynette had indicated to Bill that she was happy to provide a statement of the facts to the Association while making it clear that she was not taking sides. "I'm pleading Switzerland", she said to Bill, "I don't want to take sides or to get involved in any argument between you and Gary, but I will provide a statement outlining the facts of my involvement if required."

All of this information had been provided in the original complaint to the Association but was not investigated by James. No follow-up statement was requested from Lynette and therefore none was provided.

Later Lynette said to Bill that she would give Faz, the Association's President a call and talk through the issue with him. But she never did. Bill said that he followed this up several times with Lynette but now she "didn't want to be involved".

It seemed that Lynette was not really interested in doing anything that might require effort.

So, the investigation became a "non-investigation". The Association was not interested in investigating any of this because it knew that

Gary had done the wrong thing and that it would look bad for the Association if that became known. The Association's course of action was to just bury it.

However, despite all of the correspondence and discussion in the non-resolution of this complaint, there are two issues which surmount all others and are therefore worthy of further discussion. These are the issues relating to the Arbitration process and to the Mediation processes:

The Arbitration issue:

The first major issue which caused some considerable consternation was that relating to the decision by James to resolve this complaint by arbitration, without discussion or agreement by the parties. Certainly, Bill said that he was not asked but nevertheless he initially regarded it as a good thing.

All that Bill wanted from the investigation was an impartial and unbiased consideration of the facts, independent of either party, and arbitration by a Retired Judge seemed like a very sensible solution. Bill said that he would accept the decision of the referee (in this case the Retired Judge) and move on.

However, James was from Adelaide and the Retired Judge was from Adelaide. It was apparent that James knew the Retired Judge. This was further exacerbated when it became apparent that the Retired Judge's email address was the same as James' Solicitor. "Not seeing too much independence here", said Bill, "but this guy is a Retired Judge, so he has to be on the up and up, doesn't he?"

Bill's company was based in Sydney. Gary's company was based in Sydney. The attempted theft of Bill's IP by Gary occurred in Sydney. So, while legal jurisdictional issues between NSW and South Australia did not seem to be an issue initially, it did raise some concern, even moreso as the events proceeded.

The rules of the Association allowed for (and promoted) the use of mediation as a means of resolving issues and complaints, as is normally the case with many Associations and other industry bodies. But despite the rules of the Association mandating Mediation, James and his appointed Retired Judge dictated Arbitration. "This looks like it is set up to come to only one conclusion, and it won't be one that I will like", said Bill.

Nevertheless, Bill trusted that the process was legitimate and consequently signed the Complaints Determination Deed, but two weeks later the Retired Judge wrote to the parties referring to the Complaints Determination Deed and said in that letter "…I note from a perusal of the papers, that most of the background circumstances are not contested."

Given that the "background circumstances" were the crux of the complaint and that Bill had not seen Gary's comments on the complaint, it was very concerning that the Retired Judge could make such a statement, before any "hearing" or before any Arbitration.

Bill said that the Retired Judge has already come to his conclusion, so how could any process be considered to be remotely unbiased when the adjudicator has already made up his mind.

Following considerable consternation and correspondence from Bill's lawyers, the Retired Judge sent a letter at the end of the process and well after mediation to say that he was withdrawing from the case "… because – so it is alleged – I have demonstrated a lack of impartiality".

The Retired Judge then went on to say that "The whole of paragraph 2.1.3 of my letter to the parties, and even the one sentence plucked out of it, and apparently relied upon in the (lawyers) letter, if sensibly interpreted, is an invitation to give consideration to agreeing some background facts."

But notably, the particular letter from the Retired Judge which said that "… the background circumstances are not in contention" was several months BEFORE Gary's comments on Bill's complaint were provided, so it is inconceivable that such a statement could be made by the Retired Judge before any documentation was provided by Gary.

In addition, the "… request for the reports" were not agreed – Bill provided the reports to Gary as the Association's representative, not to Gary the consultant as Gary attested to in his Statutory Declaration later.

In summary therefore, the kindest thing that could be said about the Retired Judge is that he was gullible and he erred substantially, and then went on to document his erring further in reasonably certain terms. While this is reprehensible, it is the continued and dodged pursuit of this avenue by James from the Association that this is the most reprehensible.

It is one thing to try and "dictate the outcome" but to do it so blatantly and so obviously was just too much for Bill.

So, the process of running arbitration by using the Retired Judge had been discredited. But still James would not accept that the process that he had mandated had been found wanting.

In addition, and despite being requested to do so on several occasions, neither James nor the Retired Judge were able to produce any documentation which showed how the Retired Judge had come to the astounding conclusion that "… most of the background circumstances are not contested" as outlined in the Complaints Determination Deed.

The Solicitor for James wrote to Bill a fortnight later to say that "… the allegations of impropriety (by the Retired Judge in his pre-judging of the outcome based on no input from Gary) were without any foundation".

The Solicitor for James then said that Bill should apologise to the Retired Judge.

Bill was astounded, particularly given that the Retired Judge had, by his own letter, been found to have made statements based on NO information from Gary. He had this pointed out repeatedly, and so he sends a letter of withdrawal saying that the sentence was "plucked out" from the paragraph and that if one reads the paragraph in full then it all makes sense. But when the paragraph is read in full, it does not do that at all.

"The Arbitration process and the Retired Judge have been thoroughly discredited, but now James says it is all my fault and I should apologise," said Bill. "Unbelievable!"

The Mediation issue:

The second major issue was that of the Mediation.

As indicated previously, Mediation is defined as "…a form of alternative dispute resolution resolving disputes between two or more parties using a mediator to assist the parties to negotiate a settlement."

The mediation was undertaken on-line with software pre-loaded and pre-tested on (mostly) all of the participants computers prior to the appointed time. Bill related the process of the Mediation as follows:

- the Mediator was in her office in Sydney
- he (Bill) and his lawyers were in the offices of his lawyers in Sydney
- Gary was at his home in Sydney
- James and his Solicitor were in their office in Adelaide
- Michael was in his office in Hobart

After the initial introductions, the mediator outlined the process of having opening conversation with the option of groups going into "private rooms" for further discussion if required.

Bill recalled that the mediation was to run for 3 hours, but at the last minute Faz said he was not attending (he had previously advised by email that he would attend) and that Michael would attend in his place. But Michael did not have his software loaded, so the first 40 minutes were wasted with him loading his software and then testing it and trying to get it working and getting his IT people in to help him, etc. All the while everyone is just sitting there waiting for Michael to get organised. Bill was particularly annoyed because he was paying for two lawyers to sit and wait with him.

When everything was set up and working, Bill said that the first thing that Michael says is that he is not a Director and he cannot make a decision and that he would have to take anything back to the Board to get it approved before proceeding.

Given that the whole point of mediation, is to mediate and make appropriate decisions, preferably agreed by all parties, because Faz did not bother to turn up, or even give notice that he was not going to turn up, the whole mediation process was nullified.

Bill said the whole thing was a waste of time and designed to only look like the Association was doing something. But they were also intending to waste as much of his (Bill's) money as possible on lawyers to achieve nothing. Bill said that the whole useless exercise cost him several thousand dollars.

"So here we are, about an hour in", said Bill, "when Michael restates that he cannot make a decision, and blatantly further adds that he has not read any of the background material, but has come to the conclusion that there is 'no case to answer'."

"Everyone was gob-smacked", Bill said. "How could anyone, let alone someone who was the head of a major government department, say that he has NOT read anything but has come to the conclusion that it wasn't true." Bill was furious, "what a dill".

"But the real concern was that James and his lawyer did not refute this", said Bill. "By his own silence, they condoned this whitewashing."

By the end of the mediation, Bill had come to the conclusion that there was not going to be any resolution of his complaint, and indeed the action of James as the head of the "Investigation Committee" was grounds for further complaints.

James was not being objective and was not displaying any signs that he was at all interested in being objective.

Following the abortive mediation, Bill's lawyers wrote confidentially to Faz outlining their concerns that:

- there was no authorised Association representative at the mediation,
- there was a failure to inform the mediator that an authorised representative would not attend,
- there was a failure to consider any compromise, and
- there was a failure to engage in good faith.

Bill's lawyers pointed out that the Association had demonstrated itself to be shambolic, incompetent and unaware of its own policies and framework.

12 - And the Boot goes in

After a contemplative period following the abortive mediation process, Bill had had enough of the duplicity and obstruction by the Association, particularly with the "investigation" process run by James being so obviously and transparently a sham, designed to paint Bill as the villain and to vindicate Gary and the Association.

It had become obvious by this time that writing to Faz, the President of the Association was a waste of time because he did not respond to any correspondence. In frustration therefore, Bill decided that he would write to the Board members of the Association summarising the process that had occurred since he had made the complaint.

This then became the second complaint.

That is, Bill's letter to the Board of the Association outlined two complaint processes:

- the first complaint process being the original complaint about Gary
- the second complaint being how the Association handled / investigated the first complaint.

While the original complaint was about Gary and his nefarious activities, the second complaint was about how the Association had not provided natural justice, had tried to cover-up Gary's misdeeds and been complicit in the deceptive behaviour of James and Faz's cover-up.

So, the second complaint to the Directors outlined that the following had occurred, while attaching the chronology and relevant documents evidencing the chronology:

1. Peter the CEO changed the rules and changed the policy in a bullying, arrogant and obstructionist manner leading up to the lodging of the original complaint.

2. James changed the rules and did not adhere to the Association's complaints procedure timelines. James allowed documentation to be provided by Gary 3½ months late without censure or comment. James allowed the Association to NOT provide documentation some 5 months after being requested without censure. Faz did NOT direct the Association staff to provide documentation despite being repeatedly requested to do so.

3. James appointed a Retired Judge as an independent arbitrator and presented Bill with a Complaints Determination Deed from the Solicitor for James about the proposed arbitration process. Bill signed that Deed expecting a fair and independent process. Three weeks later the Retired Judge wrote that the "…circumstances are not contested". This was before he had read documentation provided by Gary (which James stated was provided some 3 months later) or the Association (which has still not been provided some 6 months later), before any discussion with Bill, before arbitration and without taking a statement from the witness.

4. Despite this, James repeatedly continued to insist that the Retired Judge should arbitrate the complaint, even after Bill's lawyers had repeatedly written to James and Faz pointing out that the Retired Judge was not independent and that arbitration was not in the Association' complaints procedure and that Bill had no confidence in James competence to manage an independent investigation of this complaint. Faz did not respond to this letter.

5. Faz did not attend mediation as the mediator had been advised, instead providing Michael from Hobart in his place even though Michael was not a Board member and said he had no authority to make decisions at mediation, thus invalidating the purpose of the mediation.

6. At the mediation, Michael as the Association representative, made the astounding statement that while he was new to this complaint and admitted that he had not read the background material, he said that he had investigated the complaint and found that there was no case to answer. That is, Michael attempted to "whitewash" the complaint in a most unprofessional, shameful and fact-free manner.

7. This was further exacerbated by James being silent on this statement and not contradicting Michael, thereby condoning Michael's unprofessional and untrue attempt to whitewash Bill's complaint.

8. Given the above points, it was apparent that the Association had deliberately undermined the mediation.

9. At the mediation the complaint lodged by Bill (ie the purpose of the mediation) was not discussed because most of the allotted time was spent dealing with the Association's inability to provide an authorised representative resulting in Michael's software needing to be installed and then Michael's unprofessional whitewash comments. Because of the Association's unprofessional and unethical antics at the mediation, Bill's lawyer's time was wasted which resulted in him incurring additional considerable cost for no progression of the complaint.

The actions undertaken by the Association were not in accordance with its own rules and procedures.

This was evidenced by:

- The Association continuing to propose an Arbitrator (the Retired Judge) who had declared himself to NOT be independent in his letter, stating that "... the background circumstances are not contested" when the focus of the independent arbitration process was to determine the background circumstances. One would consider the Association to not be fully competent to continue to promote such a partisan course of action to investigate a complaint which required independent investigation.

- The Chair of the Investigation Committee (James) repeatedly continuing to insist that arbitration must be followed when arbitration was NOT included in the Association Complaints rules. That is, the Association was not following its own rules. Most intelligent people would have to consider that "not following your own rules" is lacking in process, probity and professionalism.
- The Chair of the Investigation Committee (James) condoning the attempted whitewashing of the complaint by the Association representative at the mediation, thereby indicating that any notion of impartiality would be severely degraded or negated in any process involving the Chair of the Investigation Committee (James), or the Association representative, or Faz who nominated the Association representative. Most professional people would consider that this action was lacking in morals, ethics and diligence.
- All of these actions were condoned and supported by Faz who appeared to be fully informed on all activities in correspondence from James.

These actions would cause most intelligent and rational people to express concern that this complaint evaluation process had been "set-up to fail" and that it was being manipulated to come to a predetermined outcome.

Certainly, one would consider that the Association' actions in this regard may have been deceitful, dishonest, unprofessional, and tainted with illegality if this were the case, as the evidence suggested that it was.

Bill then lodged a second complaint regarding the unethical, unprofessional, and incompetent processes that the Association, Faz, James and Michael had undertaken to investigate and evaluate the first complaint.

13 - The Spineless Wimps

After the abortive complaints investigation and mediation process undertaken by James the Chair of the Complaints Committee, Bill wrote to the Board of the Association.

He summarised the facts as discussed in previous Chapters and outlined that the Association has not acted ethically or with any degree of professionalism in the conduct of the investigation or resolution of the Complaint.

Bill's letter to the Board was as follows:

"It is a shameful indictment on the Board of the Association that this has occurred and that the Board seems content to allow this to continue to occur.

"As Directors, you would be aware that all Directors of the Association are "...a director within the meaning of the Corporations Act".

"That is, each and every Director on the Association Board has a statutory responsibility comprising (amongst other things) personal and financial duties defined under the Act.

"The Association has made, and continues to make, decisions and undertakes actions under your name which do not appear to be in accordance with the Act.

"While there was a time when the Association conducted its business in a professional and ethical manner, that time now appears to have passed. Nevertheless, I recognise that some Directors may consider themselves to be ethical and professional and some may regard that they do act within the law, particularly in the context of the Corporations Act. Unfortunately, these Directors do not seem to have not been involved in the complaint resolution to date.

"Therefore, in order for Directors to avoid any severe and personal financial penalties in the future, I would respectfully suggest that:

- *each Board member carefully considers his/her exposure (liability) for decisions made by others in his/her name – at the end of the day, the buck stops with the Board, particularly with Directors, both individually and collectively;*
- *the Board resolves to progress these complaints and the matter of the unprofessional actions of the Association office bearers in an ethical, mutually respectfully and professional manner; and*
- *the Board puts in place a solid governance model to ensure that these actions do not occur again.*

"In particular, please note that this letter is addressed to the Directors of the Association, not the President. The reason for this is simple – you are the only ones left who are not tainted by the unethical and unprofessional behaviour to date and therefore probably still have the ability to make reasoned and professional decisions.

"Moreover, as Directors you are the only ones remaining that I would consider to be credible enough to make reasoned and professional decisions.

"At the end of the day, as Directors you will also "wear" the fallout / cost of this process, so logically you should make all further decisions.

"Faz, James, Michael and Peter the former the Association CEO have all repeatedly shown that they are not able to follow the Association' rules to resolve this complaint and they have undertaken practices which are not independent, not professional and not ethical.

"Indeed, a recent letter from my lawyers to James, in response to his letter, again states that I will not agree to participation in a "sham

investigation" by an arbitrator who declared 6 months ago that he had already made his determination that the "... circumstances are not in contention", apparently without reference to any facts.

"That James continues to press with this discredited and partisan arbitration process with a stated foregone conclusion by the Retired Judge is indicative of the unethical and unprofessional nature of this "complaint investigation".

"It is indeed mystifying why James pursues such a biased arbitration when this has been pointed out to him on multiple occasions. More significantly, it is further mystifying why Faz allows James to pursue this when it has also been pointed out to him on multiple occasions. Given these circumstances, one would have to wonder why both James and Faz are so intent on "railroading" this complaint to meet their preconceived and partisan outcomes.

"In conclusion, while I remain hopeful that the Association will act in a professional and ethical manner at some point, I remain sceptical that this will occur. Certainly, the evidence to date suggests that the Association have no scruples and will continue to act in an unprofessional and unethical manner.

"Nevertheless, I trust that there are some the Association Directors who can show some strength of character and finally act in a proper ethical and professional manner in order to resolve both complaints in a timely manner."

The Association did not respond to this letter, except for a 1 line note from Paul, the President Elect a fortnight later which said:

"my initial determination is that the complaint is rejected".

Paul provided no explanation, no apology, no investigation, no reason why the facts had been disregarded, no commentary at all as to why the Association had done all of the things that it has done – just that it "... is rejected".

"What a bunch of spineless wimps" said Bill, "they are not going to provide any excuse for their abhorrent actions, their illegality and their deceitful processes – they just reject it."

"And this effectively comes from the Board of the Association", said Bill, "they just stand by while all this happens and do nothing."

As Lieutenant General David Morrison, AO, retired Chief of Army said in his address to the United Nations International Women's Day Conference on 8 March 2013, **"the standard you walk past, is the standard you accept."**

Clearly the Association has walked past, and has therefore accepted that it is "business-as-usual":

- to not act in a professional and ethical manner in the resolution of any complaint
- to not follow complaints processes
- to make-up rules to favour its own perceived outcome
- to undermine mediation by not providing a Board member
- to try and to whitewash a mediation process
- to elicit the support of a Retired Judge to participate in an outcome which is knowingly untrue
- to ignore and not investigate any complaint lodged against one of its members

Given all of this, it is clear that the Association does not meet the criteria of a professional association and that it has acted with a degree of illegality.

14 - With Honesty and in good Faith – Really?

In Australia, a Director of an organisation owes a fiduciary duty to the company. That is, he or she must "act honestly, in good faith and to the best of his or her ability in the interests of the company." Section 181(1) of the Corporations Act 2001 requires that directors act "in good faith in the best interests of the corporation".

The Association in this case study is "...a not-for-profit organisation, limited by guarantee, formed as a legally constituted body as a company under the rules and regulations of the Australian Securities and Investments Commission (ASIC) in 2009."

While there is some legal debate about the pro's and con's of different company structures for industry Associations, it is clear that this Association is considered as a company in the context of the Corporations Act 2001, particularly with regard to the responsibilities of its Directors.

The Australian Institute of Company Directors provides General Duties for Directors (refer Glossary Reference 17) derived from the Corporations Act 2001 which specifies four main duties for directors:

1.   "Care and diligence – This duty requires a director to act with the degree of care and diligence that a reasonable person might be expected to show in the role (s180). A similar duty is also imposed on directors at common law. Recent court cases have emphasised this duty in relation to the approval of financial statements (Centro case) and board approval of statements issued by a company (James Hardie cases). There can also be a breach of this duty by causing a company to enter into risky transactions without any prospect of producing a benefit or where a managing director

fails to inform the board of matters which clearly should have been brought to the board's attention. The business judgment rule provides a "safe harbour" for a director in relation to a claim for a breach of care and diligence at common law or under s180.

2.   "Good faith – This duty requires a director to act in good faith in the best interests of the company and for a proper purpose (s181), including to avoid conflicts of interest, and to reveal and manage conflicts if they arise. This is a duty of fidelity and trust, known as a 'fiduciary duty' imposed by common law and a duty required in the Corporations Act 2001.

3.   "Not to improperly use position – This duty requires directors to not improperly use their position to gain an advantage for themselves or someone else, or to the detriment to the company (s182).

4.   "Not to improperly use information – This duty requires directors to not improperly use the information they gain in the course of their director duties to gain an advantage for themselves or someone else, or to the detriment to the company (s183)."

So why is this important in the context of this case study?

- The complaint tabled substantial evidence of malfeasance by Gary, the then President of the Association. When Gary used his position as President of the Association to gain an advantage for himself (by trying to steal Bill's IP to benefit his own company, not the Association), he failed to abide by Sections 182 and 183 of the Corporations Act (points 3 and 4 above).

- James, the Chair of the Complaints Committee of the Association, either by incompetence or intransience, refused to consider the evidence contained in the complaint, in the form of emails and correspondence, including Statutory Declarations from Gary and witness evidence available from Lynette. As such, James failed to abide by Section 181,

Good Faith (point 2 above) by not revealing and managing conflicts as they arose and by not trying to avoid conflicts of interest. In particular, James engaged the services of a Retired Judge in order to provide a veneer of judicial respectability across the investigation process which sadly (for James) was shot down when the Retired Judge stated that he was not impartial. That he did this suggests that not only did James not manage the conflicts of interests, but that he consciously went out of his way to create the conflicts of interest.

- Faz, the President of the Association acted improperly and incompetently in the process by not trying to resolve the escalating ineptitude of the Association and in so doing allowed James to continue to act incompetently and deceitfully. That is, Faz failed to abide by the Section 180, Care and Diligence of the Corporations Act (point 1 above).

- The Directors of the Association allowed James and Faz to continue to act incompetently and by so doing gave approval to the process. As such, the Directors of the Association did not "act honestly, in good faith and to the best of his or her ability in the interests of the company." In doing so, the Directors betrayed their fiduciary duty to the company required under Section 181(1) of the Corporations Act 2001 which requires that directors act "in good faith in the best interests of the corporation" at all times (point 1 above).

15 - ... and so it ends

A footnote in the history of this story is that a new CEO was appointed to the Association some 15 months after the resignation of Peter, the previous CEO.

"I know Tony, the new CEO", said Bill, "and when I knew him a few years ago before he moved to Perth, he was a man of integrity and principle. Perhaps there is some hope that he can repair some of the damage wrought by the Association onto the industry, as well as to sort out this issue".

However, after a number of phone calls and many emails, it became apparent that Tony had been "captured" by the "power group" in the Association and was likely to be under pressure to block any further action or to professionally act on the two complaints.

For some weeks Bill and Tony had several conversations about Tony's continued lack of understanding of the issues relating to the unprofessional conduct of the Association embodied in the complaint. Bill continued to press Tony to read the correspondence and the evidence and to talk to the witness, but Tony continued to insist that he wanted to stand back and let an investigator do the investigating.

Bill sent an email after several of these discussions saying "Tony, while I can appreciate that you are trying to remain outside of all of this, as CEO the buck stops with you. All the rest of the power group, including the Board, have been discredited, so that leaves only you".

Unfortunately, while Tony did try and arrange some meetings to progress some issues, nothing really happened. He continued to refuse to read the correspondence and evidence or to speak to Lynette the witness. His excuse continued to be that he wanted to stand back and let an investigator do the investigation.

"An admiral sentiment" Bill said, "but the Association then blocks and delays the appointment of an investigator. Particularly one that really is independent and not trying to do a stitch-up job like James did".

So, Tony continued to say that "the complaint has not been investigated, so we cannot take action against Gary" who was still a member of the Association and still being promoted on the Association website. But he would not arrange for anyone to investigate the complaint, so it all became a circular argument.

However, Tony did make an attempt to get an investigator from another Association involved at Bill's suggestion, but it was obvious after several months this was just cosmetic. Tony continued to refuse to do anything that would address the issues and:

- refused to get an independent mediator or lawyer involved to review the evidence;
- refused to read the evidence and the documentation; and
- refused to talk to Lynette, the witness.

But Tony continued to promote Gary, the past President of the Association who tried to steal the IP. Tony refused to remove Gary from the Association's web site and refused to start the process to expel Gary from the membership.

In fact, Tony said he felt sorry for Gary and told Bill that "Gary has been doing it tough".

Bill was astounded by this comment from Tony. These were unbelievable comments from the CEO of the Association to express concern for the person who had tried to steal IP under the cover of representing the Association while blocking all attempts to properly and professionally address this issue.

Tony had refused to do anything, except to think up excuses for why nothing had happened and now he was "feeling sorry" for the person who had tried to steal the IP in the first place. It was now very obvious to Bill that Tony was just stonewalling, as the Association had done for the last 20 months.

By Tony feeling sorry for Gary, in effect he was blaming Bill for reporting the attempted theft of the IP.

That is, Tony was "victim blaming".

There is an old saying that "… the fish starts to rot from the head" and here was proof that the head was rotting. Tony was the CEO, and therefore the administrative head of the Association, and he was feeling sorry for Gary the thief while blaming the Bill the victim for reporting the theft. Faz, as President, was the elected head of the Association and had long a history of not doing anything to act properly and professionally in trying to resolve these issues.

This confirmed that the Association was without any moral or professional fibre.

In Tony's mind it was Bill's fault for reporting Gary's malfeasance, not Gary's fault for trying to steal the IP from Bill in the first place. This revelation was confirmed a week later when Tony sent an email to Bill saying that the delays were largely Bill's fault.

Bill was stunned by this assertion from Tony.

To Bill this seemed to be just one more attempt by the Association to "shoot the messenger" and discredit Bill as part of the stonewalling pattern by the Association.

This was just more of the same previous attempts to do nothing by the Association.

But this set of emails from Tony did confirm to Bill that there was an "unfortunate pattern" occurring with the Association – that they agree to a process to finalise an outcome and then set about to either destroy or compromise that process.

Tony was just the most recent person to take up this role, following on from James and Faz.

That is, the Association had tried to destroy or compromise the process a number of times over the previous 20 months, when:

- the initial agreement to do an independent investigation did not happen for the entire time (over some 20 months) that the investigation period occurred;
- the promise to appoint an independent adjudicator to an arbitration process was aborted when he (the Retired Judge) declared that he was not independent;
- the promise to conduct professional mediation was aborted when the Association decision maker did not bother to attend;
- further, the promise to conduct a professional mediation was aborted when the Association representative tried to whitewash the mediation; and
- repeated requests and promises to provide information and documentation about how various Association representatives came to conclusions were not provided.

Then Tony had the temerity to tell Bill that it was all his fault.

That is, after 20 months from when the complaint was lodged, nothing has happened.

The Board collectively did nothing and the Directors appeared to just hope that it would all go away.

The Association has shown by its actions that it was and continued to be unprofessional, unethical and without any management processes in place to rectify the attempted theft of the IP nor to put in place measures to ensure that this did not happen again.

But to Bill the final straw was when Tony said he felt sorry for Gary and that "Gary has been doing it tough". This was the final insult.

That was when Bill decided that some proactive action was required.

LinkedIn Posts

Bill decided to take things into his own hands and posted on LinkedIn an outline of the story. This then became the start of an ongoing commentary under the heading of "What would you do if someone tried to steal your IP".

Surprisingly, within a day Tony suddenly found that he could actually make a phone call to Lynette and talk about the events surrounding the attempted theft of Bill's IP by Gary.

Suddenly it all became easy for Tony.

Tony then emailed Bill about his conversation with Lynette. *"Lynette was regularly speaking with both Gary and yourself at the time of the events occurring and did see most of the emails exchanged. While I got the impression she would prefer not to be drawn in as a witness unless there was absolutely no other option, she did confirm your statements but made the point that she cannot be relied upon too heavily because of the amount of time that has elapsed since the original event."*

So, while Lynette's discussion with Tony did validate Bill's testimony, he was still extremely disappointed.

Bill replied to Tony "You've finally spoken to Lynette after 3 months of me asking you to talk to her and after 20 months of the Association being asked but not doing it. 20 months!! Now you tell me that she "can't recall". How very convenient.".

Bill went on "Perhaps if the incompetent Association "investigator" had done his job 20 months ago, Lynette's memories would have been fresh. Even better would have been if he further done his job and got a STATEMENT. I wonder why that didn't happen."

To say that Bill's anger was white-hot would be an understatement.

Clearly James, the incompetent Association "investigator" had not spoken to Lynette because he did not want the truth to come out which might contradict his carefully crafted story that it was all Bill's fault, which he could then use to discredit Bill.

Sadly, that was the same theme that Tony carried further in his subsequent emails. Blame Bill! Shoot the messenger! It's all Bill's fault for being the whistle-blower. Poor Gary is doing it tough.

But Tony went one step further and made a thinly veiled threat against Bill that the Association would commence legal action if Bill continued to make posts on LinkedIn.

Bill's response went along the lines of "go ahead, make my day".

But Tony was just bluffing, more wimpish behaviour from a failed leader of a unprofessional Association without a moral backbone trying to threaten and bully in the hope of making it go away.

Around this time, Bill also received several "exploratory" calls and emails from "friendlies" of the Association trying to trap him into naming the Association and the individuals involved, obviously in the hope that this could be used to instigate legal proceedings against Bill.

Tony was only continuing the intimidatory process started by James and condoned by Faz over the last 20 months.

Again, the conclusion of the Association was that it was all Bill's fault. It has to be Bill's fault because the Association was not going to undertake a proper and competent investigation, nor enter into sensible conversation with Bill in an attempt to resolve this issue.

Tony had the temerity to say that he felt sorry for Gary. "Gary's been doing it tough" Tony said.

Of course, if Gary had acted professionally and ethically in the first place and not tried to steal Bill's IP, then this whole process would not have happened, and Gary would not have had to "do it tough".

So instead of Tony blaming Gary for being unprofessional and unethical, he blames Bill for blowing the whistle on Gary' attempted theft and then further goes on to blame Bill for expecting the Association to do something about it, particularly something professional.

The mysterious disappearing LinkedIn Profiles

So while that's where this story might end, a codicil to this saga is that the LinkedIn posts made by Bill under the title of "What would you do if someone tried to steal your IP" had an unexpected reaction – most of the Directors of the Association began to delete or hide their LinkedIn profiles.

That is, the Directors hid their profiles so that they could not be found on LinkedIn and by doing so, they were trying to just "quietly slip away" and hide, something like a child might do when hiding behind a curtain when he/she does something wrong.

In hiding their LinkedIn profiles, the Directors exposed their culpability in this sordid saga.

Clearly, the Directors felt ashamed of their actions and wanted to hide. The Directors were culpable and ashamed that they had stood by and allowed the Association to act in the unprofessional and unethical manner that they did.

In particular, Faz and James, the two main protagonists (villains) of the Association went to some extraordinary lengths to make sure that they were unable to be found on LinkedIn.

Faz, the "show pony" of the Association, who was always highly visible on LinkedIn, the Association website and in all publications, was now nowhere to be seen.

From the start, all that Bill had wanted was a retraction from Gary that his IP was not going to be used by Gary to support Gary's business. An "optional extra" would have been to receive an apology.

Later Bill said he wanted some reimbursement of his legal fees after it became obvious that the Association was undertaking delaying tactics so that Bill would run up an enormous legal debt trying to fight the Association.

At no stage did Bill talk about damages inflicted by the Association who tried at some length to discredit Bill – perhaps he should have threatened this.

Bill did contemplate taking the Association to court. His legal team briefed a Barrister who drafted papers to lodge in the Federal Court. But it became more obvious as time went on that this was a route which had no end, would come at a considerable cost and would produce no tangible or satisfactory outcomes.

If Bill "won", there would likely be no settlement and the wimps at the Association would simply say that they had changed their processes and that all issues had now been remedied.

Plan A

So, after it became very apparent that the Association had no intention of investigating the complaint or otherwise acting in a professional manner with regard to the complaint, Bill decided to revert to Plan A and to document in a book:

- the Association's (then) President trying to steal the IP of a member of the Association;
- the Association's (then) President "doubling down" on this attempted theft by saying (in a Statutory Declaration) that he would use the stolen IP in discussions with other parties;
- the Association's (then) President fabricating the events in his statement of evidence;
- the Association actively covering up the attempted theft;
- the Association actively blocking all attempts at any resolution of the complaint;
- the Association not investigating the complains and not seeking witness evidence;

- the Association promoting Arbitration when that was not allowed under the rules
- the Association arranging a "stitch up" by a complaint Retired Judge;
- the Association trying to whitewash the complaint at Mediation;
- the Association not bothering to send a person capable of making a decision to the mediation;
- the Association's current President not responding to any correspondence or providing any statement to facilitate the complaint resolution;
- the Association's new CEO repeatedly refusing to consider the evidence or talk to the witness; and
- the Association's new CEO blaming Bill for the past President "doing it tough" because he attempted to steal and use Bill's IP.

In the end, this saga of Bill's complaint to the Association is a sad and sorry epitaph which shows the lack of integrity, lack of professionalism and lack of proper governance processes of this industry Association.

In a recent interview for a major industry magazine, Faz the (now outgoing) President of the Association recounted that some of the significant accomplishments of his administration included "restructuring our board governance and accountability procedures" and "initiating a constitutional review", all the while extolling the vision of his leadership.

Faz's hypocrisy in making these statements while:

- ignoring his responsibilities by covering up Gary's theft, and
- failing to professionally manage the complaint process,

… showed that the Association under his leadership had become truly unprofessional and broken.

Anecdotally, it is understood that theft of IP is not uncommon in other industry Associations, with multiple calls and emails resulting from the LinkedIn posts suggesting that this might be the case.

So, the moral of this story is that it did not need to happen.

Had Gary simply signed the original Statutory Declaration when he was first asked, Bill would have accepted it, and everyone would have gone on with their lives. Had he even mumbled a half-apology, that would have been accepted.

As it was, Gary's refusal to sign the Statutory Declaration showed deliberate intent to do wrong. Then, when he changed the words in the Statutory Declaration to say that he would continue to use Bill's IP showed that this was more than just a deliberate intent to do wrong.

This showed malfeasance.

Gary clearly intended to steal Bill's IP and to use it in his own consulting company in competition with Bill. In hindsight Gary was only stopped from doing this because of the furore caused by Bill.

But the real tragedy was the cover-up by the Association in trying to protect Gary.

That resulted in a firestorm of processes (at some considerable cost to both sides) which just showed how incompetent and unprofessional the Association really was.

As is often the case, the cover-up became worse than the original crime.

16 - Roadmap to Change

The issues discussed in this book can largely be grouped together as a lack of corporate governance, overlaid by a lack of integrity and professionalism by the Association and the office bearers of the Association, principally Gary, James, Faz and to a lesser extent Michael, Paul and Tony.

In hindsight, the Association management team should have had oversight of Gary's activities so that the issue of the attempted theft of Bill's IP could have been "nipped in the bud" when it first occurred. This did not occur and so it was left to Bill and Gary to argue over issues that should not have had to be argued about.

This clearly resulted in Gary "digging his heels in" over the issue and refusing to sign the original Statutory Declaration, likely out of belligerence and deviousness.

The Association management team should have had a proper process in place so that when discussion about the complaint was first mooted, there was a qualifying process to ensure that it did not escalate into a formal complaint. This did not happen.

Indeed, Peter the former CEO belligerently "dared" Bill to lodge the complaint, otherwise "… the matter would be closed". In those early days, Bill wanted this to be resolved in a low-key manner as possible but only lodged an official complaint because he was goaded to do so by Peter.

James, the Complaints Chair clearly had no training in how to resolve complaints nor any training on how to act within any probity constraints, continually changing the rules when he should have not been allowed to do this. Again, this was also a governance issue which should have been overseen by the Association management team, particularly when Bill's lawyers continually wrote to Faz stating that this was occurring.

In hindsight, James was clearly incompetent in the role of Complaints Chair and even lacked the most basic skill required of this position – to act honestly and with integrity. This was surprising given that he ran his own mid-size company in Adelaide and (one would assume) had some experience with honesty, competency and probity in his role as company director.

Faz, the Association President did not take the matter seriously and had no oversight of either the former CEO or the Complaints Chair and did not appear to be interested in having any oversight. This was exacerbated by his not responding to any correspondence or bothering to turn up at the mediation, one of the few opportunities to defuse this issue and resolve it with a semi-amicable outcome.

It was also obvious that Faz was really just a "show pony" only interested in promoting himself at conferences and not at all interested in doing "the hard yards" as an Association President in sorting the complaint out or in keeping James on track as the Complaints Chair.

In summary, the lack of any formal processes exacerbated the already fractious relationship between Bill and the Association, resulting in both sides spending many tens-of-thousands of dollars in legal fees to fight that which was becoming an out-of-control process.

The outcome of all of this was an (apparent) desire by the Association to adopt a "win at all cost" approach, exemplified by the hiring of the Retired Judge to:

- "stitch up" the process by arbitration when arbitration was not allowed under the rules in any event; and to
- provide a veneer of judicial respectability over a process which, by that time, had largely been tainted and discredited.

When it further became apparent that the lawyer of the Complaints Chair and the Retired Judge shared the same offices and the same email accounts (even without the Retired Judge pre-judging the outcome before all statements were presented) it became totally untenable.

Unfortunately, the outcome of this lack of acumen and professionalism by the Association in general and by James in particular, led to the desire to discredit Bill by any means.

That is, this became a process to discredit Bill and the complaint that he had lodged because they did not want to hear the message contained in the complaint or to address any of the underlying issues.

In effect, this became a process to "shoot the whistle-blower".

17 – The Final Word

As the title of this book indicates, this is a true case study which occurred in a major industry Association in IT / GIS in Australia between April 2017 and mid-2020. All of the events cited in this book actually happened and are as documented in brief in this book and in the documentation held by Bill and the Association. All events are backed up by emails, correspondence by lawyers and recordings of meetings.

So, what does this true story tell the reader about industry Associations in general and this Association in particular?

How can the reader move forward, knowing that this incident happened in an Association of which he/she (that is, the reader) may currently be a member?

Firstly, I want to stress that this case study does NOT suggest that this happens in ALL industry Associations. It does however happen in a lot of them, to a smaller or larger extent.

Since I have been on this journey of discovery since April 2017, I have anecdotally found that this type of IP theft in Associations occurs regularly, and that the Associations involved generally do nothing about it and just dismiss the incident or try to intimidate or belittle the complainant (if a complaint is made).

The IP that is stolen might be a presentation that has been created about a project or concept which is "taken over" by another member (usually a superior) who then goes on to present and claim the work of others as their own, in some cases winning accolades for work which was not his/hers, and which contains other people's IP.

It might be research which has been requested for the industry Association but then used by the requestor personally, such as the case documented in this book.

It might be a fund-raising concept that a member may have designed and raised in a Committee but is then taken over by the Committee Chair as their own personal idea to curry favour with Delegates and Sponsors or to "prop up" their failing ego's.

Given that this is not an uncommon occurrence, are there signs that the reader can look for that might suggest that something is not going the way it should, and that their proprietary IP might be at risk?

As an Association member, are you prepared to be a "change agent" and "change maker" and try to put in place processes which may correct these actions when they arise?

When the opportunity arises to be on an Association Committee or to be an office bearer of an Association, would you rather follow proper procedures or do nothing should you become aware that this type of action is occurring.

If the proper procedures are not documented in a manual, would you do the "right thing" and set one up.

Would you be an "enabler" rather than a "passenger" or "blocker" ?

Would you be honest and professional or be unprofessional and unethical like Gary, James, Faz and the Association?

Glossary / References

The following references and definitions are used within this book as appropriate:

Reference 1 – Corporate GIS – Trading name for CorpGIS Pty Ltd – refer www.corporategis.com.au

Reference 2 – Professionalism – refer https://www.merriam-webster.com/dictionary/professionalism

Reference 3 – "Professionalism in the Information and Communications Technology Industry", ANU Press – refer https://press.anu.edu.au/publications/series/practical-ethics-public-policy/professionalism-information-and-communication

Reference 4 – Information Technology Professionals Association – refer https://www.itpa.org.au/code-of-ethics/

Reference 5 – *IP Australia* – refer https://www.ipaustralia.gov.au/

Reference 6 – Intellectual Property (IP) refer https://www.merriam-webster.com/dictionary/intellectual%20property

Reference 7 – Digital Rights Management (DRM) – refer https://www.macmillandictionary.com/dictionary/british/digital-rights-management

Reference 8 – The Ethics Centre – refer https://www.ethics.org.au

Reference 9 – Consultant – refer https://www.merriam-webster.com/dictionary/consultant

Reference 10 – Consultant – refer https://en.wikipedia.org/wiki/Consultant

Reference 11 – "Trust me, I'm an IT Consultant", Bruce Douglas 2019 – available from https://www.amazon.com.au/Trust-Me-Consultant-Bruce-Douglas-ebook/dp/B07SSSN15C

Reference 12 – "Achieving Business Success with GIS", Bruce Douglas 2008 – available from https://onlinelibrary.wiley.com/doi/book/10.1002/9780470985595

Reference 13 – Nearmap – refer https://www.nearmap.com/au/en

Reference 14 – Creative Commons – refer https://creativecommons.org/about/program-areas/open-data/

Reference 15 – Arbitration – refer https://www.disputescentre.com.au/arbitration.

Reference 16 – Mediation – refer https://www.disputescentre.com.au/mediation/

Reference 17 – Australian Institute of Company Directors – refer https://aicd.companydirectors.com.au/-/media/cd2/resources/director-resources/director-tools/pdf/05446-6-2-duties-directors_general-duties-directors_a4-web.ashx

Appendix

The following are redacted images of key documents:

Item 1

The following is an email from Gary, the then President of the Association, on the 27 April 2017 about an hour after Bill had provided a copy of his reports to Gary in his (Gary's) capacity as President of the Association for the Association to use.

Note that this email from Gary does not mention the Association, for which the reports were requested. However, the second Statutory Declaration dated 5 June 2017 does say at point 3 (following) that he received the IP in his capacity as President of the Association.

That is, this email is Gary's attempt to steal Bill's IP so that he could use it in his own consulting business, not for Association business.

From:

Sent: Thursday, 27 April, 2017 10:22 AM

To:

Subject: Re: Reports - email 2 of 2

Hi

It has been a while since I looked at this report. I forgot how absolutely comprehensive it was!

I find it a shame that it has "died". I am considering reviving it, if you are happy to come to some IP / collaboration agreement. I don't want to steal your IP, but I also need to find a way to make it work for me. The market has changed somewhat, and I will have to change many of the parameters. But keeping things in line with the work you did will enable me to develop an historical comparison base. Don't have any real answers.

How about the following:

1. Acknowledgement in the report of your history, etc.
2. Some shared allocation of responsibility of report generation.
3. Some shared allocation of funds generated from reports sold.
4. Other suggestions

Cheers

Item 2

The following is a copy of the Statutory Declaration which Gary, the then President of the Association, signed on 28 April 2017.

Note that the oath Gary is declaring is very different to the oath in the Statutory Declaration which he was asked to sign by Bill and was signed some 6 weeks later (refer Item 3 overpage).

In this first Statutory Declaration, Gary is saying, on oath, that he will continue to use Bill's IP and that he will be the "gatekeeper" between third parties (note that parties is plural) and Bill, even though the reports are Bill's IP and Bill has not agreed to this arrangement.

Statutory Declaration

OATHS ACT 1900, NSW, NINTH SCHEDULE

I, ▮▮▮▮▮▮▮▮▮▮▮▮▮▮, of ▮▮▮▮▮▮▮▮▮▮▮▮▮▮▮▮
[name of declarant]   [residence]

do hereby solemnly declare and affirm that I have removed all copies of reports sent to
me by ▮▮▮▮▮▮▮▮ as requested. I have no digital or printed copies of any of
these reports, nor do I have access to any of these anywhere.

Having seen the reports, I will refer to these in my discussion with external parties, and
if required will ask these individuals to contact ▮▮▮▮▮▮ directly should they need
further information.

....

....

....

....

....

[the facts to be stated according to the declarant's knowledge, belief, or information, severally]

And I make this solemn declaration, as to the matter (or matters) aforesaid, according
to the law in this behalf made – and subject to the punishment by law provided for any
wilfully false statement in any such declaration.

Declared at: Thornleigh NSW on 28 April 2017
              [place]   [date]

                                          ▮▮▮▮▮▮▮▮
                                          [signature of declarant]

in the presence of an authorised witness, who states:

I, ▮▮▮▮▮▮▮▮▮▮▮▮▮▮▮▮
   [name of authorised witness]   [qualification of authorised witness]

certify the following matters concerning the making of this statutory declaration by the
who made it: [* please cross out any text that does not apply]

1. *I saw the face of the person OR *I did not see the face of the person because the person
    was wearing a face covering, but I am satisfied that the person had a special justification
    for not removing the covering, and

2. *I have known the person for at least 12 months OR *I have confirmed the person's identity using an
    identification document and the document I relied on was ▮▮▮▮▮▮▮▮▮▮ .
                                          [describe identification document relied on]

▮▮▮▮▮▮▮▮▮▮   28 | 4 | 17
[signature of authorised witness]   [date]

Statutory Declaration 1, signed 28 April 2017

Item 3

The following is a copy of the second Statutory Declaration signed by Gary, the then President of the Association, on 5th June 2017, some 6 weeks after being requested to sign this on 28 April 2017, and instead signing the first (altered) Statutory Declaration (shown in Item 2 above).

Note the third point in this Statutory Declaration. Gary agrees that the IP was provided to him in his capacity as President of the Association, not as a Consultant running his own company.

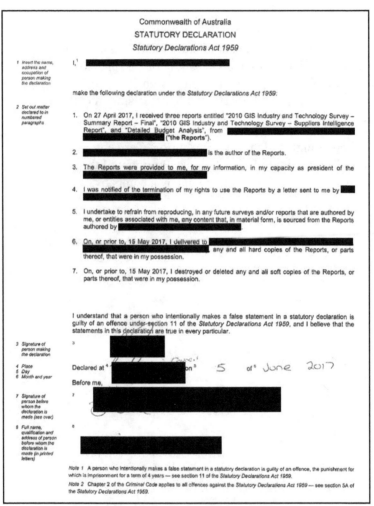

Commonwealth of Australia

STATUTORY DECLARATION

Statutory Declarations Act 1959

<table>
<tr><td>1 Insert the name, address and occupation of person making the declaration</td><td>I,¹ ████████████████████████</td></tr>
</table>

make the following declaration under the *Statutory Declarations Act 1959*:

<table>
<tr><td>2 Set out matter declared to in numbered paragraphs</td><td>

1. On 27 April 2017, I received three reports entitled "2010 GIS Industry and Technology Survey – Summary Report – Final", "2010 GIS Industry and Technology Survey – Suppliers Intelligence Report", and "Detailed Budget Analysis", from ████████████████████ ("the Reports").

2. ████████████████████████ is the author of the Reports.

3. The Reports were provided to me, for my information, in my capacity as president of the ████████████████████

4. I was notified of the termination of my rights to use the Reports by a letter sent to me by ████

5. I undertake to refrain from reproducing, in any future surveys and/or reports that are authored by me, or entities associated with me, any content that, in material form, is sourced from the Reports authored by ████████████████.

6. On, or prior to, 15 May 2017, I delivered to ████████████████████████ ████████████████, any and all hard copies of the Reports, or parts thereof, that were in my possession.

7. On, or prior to, 15 May 2017, I destroyed or deleted any and all soft copies of the Reports, or parts thereof, that were in my possession.

</td></tr>
</table>

I understand that a person who intentionally makes a false statement in a statutory declaration is guilty of an offence under section 11 of the *Statutory Declarations Act 1959*, and I believe that the statements in this declaration are true in every particular.

<table>
<tr><td>3 Signature of person making the declaration</td><td>³ ████████████████</td></tr>
<tr><td>4 Place
5 Day
6 Month and year</td><td>Declared at ⁴ ████████████ on ⁵ 5   of⁶ June 2017

Before me,</td></tr>
<tr><td>7 Signature of person before whom the declaration is made (see over)</td><td>⁷ ████████████████████████</td></tr>
<tr><td>8 Full name, qualification and address of person before whom the declaration is made (in printed letters)</td><td>⁸ ████████████████████</td></tr>
</table>

Note 1 A person who intentionally makes a false statement in a statutory declaration is guilty of an offence, the punishment for which is imprisonment for a term of 4 years — see section 11 of the *Statutory Declarations Act 1959*.

Note 2 Chapter 2 of the *Criminal Code* applies to all offences against the *Statutory Declarations Act 1959* — see section 5A of the *Statutory Declarations Act 1959*.

Statutory Declaration 2, signed 5 June 2017

Item 4

The following is an extract from the letter sent by the Retired Judge after the Complaint Determination Deed was signed and BEFORE a statement was provided by Gary, the past President of the Association and before any statement was requested from Lynette, the witness.

2.1 Particulars of Misconduct and Response ·

2.1.1 I direct that the complainant be prepared to particularise and characterise the conduct which he claims was breached by both Respondents. In other words the Complainant needs to assert that the conduct amounted to a breach of a particular clause in the Governing Documents. Further, the Complainant should identify what penalty he seeks. (n.b. the possible penalties are outlined in Clause 8.3 of the Constitution.)

2.1.2 So too I direct the two respondents to articulate a response to the Complaint as particularised. Some time may be necessary for this to happen. I will detail a timetable for the provision of such particulars and the response hereto.

2.1.3 Further to this, I note from a perusal of the papers that most of the background circumstances are not contested. For instance the fact of the request for the reports and the confrontation that followed appear to be agreed and perhaps the parties could give consideration to there being an agreed factual background.

www.ingramcontent.com/pod-product-compliance
Lightning Source LLC
LaVergne TN
LVHW051656050326
832903LV00032B/3838